IRELAND
Legends & Folklore

IRELAND
Legends & Folklore

AOIFE CURRAN

METRO BOOKS
New York

METRO BOOKS
New York

An Imprint of Sterling Publishing
387 Park Avenue South
New York, NY 10016

METRO BOOKS and the distinctive Metro Books logo
are trademarks of Sterling Publishing Co., Inc.

ISBN 978-1-4351-4516-0

For information about custom editions, special sales,
and premium and corporate purchases, please contact
Sterling Special Sales at 800-805-5489 or
specialsales@sterlingpublishing.com.

Manufactured in China

2 4 6 8 10 9 7 5 3

www.sterlingpublishing.com

CONTENTS

INTRODUCTION 6

INTRODUCTION

The first-known human settlements in Ireland were established in around 8000 BC, when Mesolithic hunter-gatherers immigrated here from continental Europe. Few archeological traces remain of this group but their descendants and later arrivals, particularly from the Iberian Peninsula, were responsible for major Neolithic sites such as Newgrange (*see also* page 166). On the arrival of St. Patrick and other Christian missionaries in the early to mid-5th century AD, Christianity began to subsume the indigenous Celtic religion, a process that was completed by the year 600.

From around AD 800, more than a century of Viking invasions wrought havoc upon the monastic culture and on the island's

various regional dynasties, yet both of these institutions proved strong enough to survive and assimilate the invaders. The coming, in 1169, of Cambro-Norman mercenaries under Richard de Clare, 2nd Earl of Pembroke, nicknamed Strongbow, marked the beginning of more than 700 years of direct English and later British involvement in Ireland.

ABOVE: St. Patrick himself is said to have created the Irish Celtic cross by laying the Latin Christian cross on top of the more ancient Pagan circle symbolizing the sun.

LEFT: The banshee in one of her guises as an old crone. To hear her keening is a warning of an impending death.

LEFT: The leprechaun is a mythical creature with origins stretching back to before the arrival of the Celts. He is the fairy shoemaker of Ireland and one of the island's original inhabitants.

BELOW: Newgrange, and the wider Brú na Bóinne Neolithic complex, were regarded by some as the abode of the supernatural Tuatha Dé Danann, while others saw them as the burial mounds of the ancient kings of Tara.

The Irish are famous for their way with words and distinguished literary tradition, and the long and eventful history of Ireland has been considerably enlivened by its ancient mythology and folklore which, fortunately, has remained largely unaffected in this modern age, and remains very much alive in the minds of her people. Stories continue to be told around the fire, usually with the storyteller enjoying a "wee drop o' the black stuff to whet his whistle."

Early tales were part of an oral tradition of storytelling until they came to be written

INTRODUCTION

down by Irish Christian scribes. Irish families still have their individual tales to tell, which are added to and embroidered and passed down from generation to generation. Fantastic tales of magical fairy castles abound, and of fearsome shape-changing hags, or pookas, which inhabit the night and leave a trail of mayhem and mischief in their wake.

The Tuatha Dé Danann were the mysterious god-like people of ancient Ireland, and were the race most closely connected with the megalithic sites of Ireland, such as Brú na Bóinne (Palace of the Boyne). Stories of the Tuatha Dé Danann survive and are repeated to this day. The ancient Celts referred to them as the Sidhe, the spirit-race of ancient Ireland, and believed them to be Ireland's original fairy folk.

One of the most popular fairy creatures of Irish folklore is the leprechaun (*leipreachán*), who takes the form of an old man, no taller than a small child and clad in a red or green coat. Leprechauns are fairy shoemakers, who also enjoy mischief-making, and the light tap of their hammers can sometimes be heard. Most leprechauns have a pouch of gold that anyone catching them can possibly keep. But to get the gold, the leprechaun's captor must never look away or the leprechaun will vanish into thin air. Like other fairy creatures, leprechauns are said to have links with the Tuatha Dé Danann, the "peoples of the goddess Danu," of Irish mythology.

RIGHT: According to mythology, the River Boyne was the creation of the goddess Bóann, the daughter of Delbáeth, son of Elatha, of the Tuatha Dé Danann.

Then there are the blood-curdling tales of the dreaded banshee, usually regarded as a harbinger of death, and how her piercing cry can be heard on dark, cold and lonely nights. People will swear they have heard her keening, and how they hoped against hope that it was only the wind in the trees and not a dire

warning that one of their kin would be departing in the coach of death (*coiste bordhar*).

Stories of banshees were also told in America in the late 18th century, the most persistant of these coming from Edgecombe County, North Carolina, where they were ghouls rather than presagers of death.

To this day, a misbehaving child will often be told by a parent that, if they refuse to mend their ways, the fairies or the Sidhe (pronounced shee), the remnants of the ancient Tuatha Dé Dannan, will come and spirit them away, leaving a changeling child in their place.

CHAPTER ONE
THE FOUR CYCLES OF IRISH MYTHOLOGY

Tales of epic adventures, battles, voyages, invasions, and of gods and heroes are contained in four cycles of Irish myths and legends: the Mythological Cycle, the Fenian Cycle, the Ulster Cycle and the Historical Cycle.

THE MYTHOLOGICAL CYCLE

The Mythological Cycle tells of the gods of the distant past and the origins of the Irish people, one of the most popular stories being "The Children of Lir," the tragic tale of a woman, driven by jealousy to turn her four stepchildren into swans. Other tales include "The Wooing of Étain" *(Tochmarc Étaíne),* "The Battle of Maige Tuireadh *(Cath Maige Tuireadh)*" and "The Dream of Aengus."

The Tuatha Dé Danann were the mysterious god-like people of ancient Ireland, and were the race most closely associated with the ancient megalithic sites of Ireland, such as Newgrange and Brú na Bóinne (Palace of the Boyne). Stories of the

Tuatha Dé Danann are many and varied and have a magical appeal which has not been lost in the mists of time. Danu is usually described as the mother

OPPOSITE: The story of "The Children of Lir," and of how they were turned into swans, is one of the most famous stories of the Irish Mythological Cycle.

ABOVE: An ancient standing stone at Newgrange, County Meath.

OVERLEAF: Newgrange, older than Stonehenge and the great pyramids of Giza, is just one monument within the Neolithic Brú na Bóinne (Palace of the Boyne) UNESCO World Heritage Site.

of the Tuatha Dé Danaan and by many sources as the mother of all the gods and goddesses of the Celtic Pantheon.

The Tuatha Dé Danann are thought to have derived from the pre-Christian deities of Ireland. When the surviving stories were written, Ireland had been Christian for centuries, and the Tuatha Dé Danaan were represented as mortal kings, queens and heroes of the distant past; there are many clues, however, as to their former divine status. They also share many parallels across the Celtic world: Nuada equates with the British god Nodens; Lugh is a reflex of the pan-Celtic deity Lugus; Tuireann is related to the Gaulish Taranis; Ogma to Ogmios; the Badb to Catubodua.

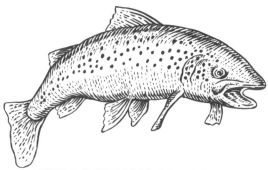

THE DROWNING OF BOANN

Bóann or Bóinn is the Irish goddess of the Boyne, a river in Leinster, and was said to be the daughter of Delbáeth, son of Elada, of the Tuatha Dé Danann. Various sources give her husband's name as Nechtan, Elemar or Nuada, while her lover is the Dagda, by whom she has a son, Aengus. In order to hide their affair, the Dagda made the sun stand still for nine months, with the result that Aengus was conceived, gestated and born in one day.

Bóann is said to have created the River Boyne. Though forbidden to by her husband, Nechtan, Bóann approached the magic Well of Segais (Well of Wisdom), which was surrounded by hazel trees, the nuts from which fell into the well where they were eaten by speckled salmon (which, along with hazelnuts, represent wisdom in Irish mythology).

Bóann challenged the power of the well by passing three times around it to the left, as was customary in several of the ancient incantations. Upon the completion of the third round, the charm was broken, the spring rose, and three enormous waves burst over her, flowed forth in five streams and drowned her. She did not die, however, but lost an arm, a leg and an eye in her battle with the well. She then fled toward the sea to hide her deformity, but the waters, now loosened from their source, still followed till she reached the Inbher, or present mouth of the river, and was swept on the rushing waters of the Boyne into the sea.

The five streams of wisdom that flowed forth from this well are the five senses: taste, smell, feeling, sight and hearing. Bóann suffered the Druidic death of drowning, but because she could not truly die (being a spirit and a goddess of the Sidhe), she gained wisdom as the waters swept her away, creating the River Boyne in the process.

ABOVE BOTH: Salmon and hazelnuts represent wisdom in Irish mythology.

OPPOSITE: The River Boyne is named after the goddess Bóann, who drowned in a surge of water from the Well of Wisdom, creating the River Boyne in the process.

THE DAGDA'S HARP

It is said that there were two quite different races of people in Ireland: one with long, dark hair and dark eyes, called the Fomorians (Fomoire), who carried long slender spears made of bronze when they fought, and another which was golden-haired and blue-eyed, and which carried short, blunt, heavy spears of a dull metal.

The golden-haired people had a great chieftain who was also a kind of high priest, called the Dagda, who possessed a wonderful magic harp. The harp was beautiful in form, mighty in size, and made of a rare wood, ornamented with gold and jewels; it made wonderful music which only the Dagda could evoke. When the men were going out to battle, the Dagda would set up his magic harp, pluck the strings, and a war song would ring out to inspire every warrior to buckle on his armor, brace his knees, and shout, "Forth to the fight!" Then, when the men returned from the battle, weary and wounded, the Dagda would take his harp and strike a few chords, and as the magic music filled the air, every man would forget his weariness and the pain of his wounds, and think of the honor won, and of the comrade who had died beside him, and of returning to his wife and children. Then the song would swell even louder, and every warrior would remember only the glory he had helped to win for the king; and each man would rise at the

great tables, his cup in his hand, and shout, "Long live the King!"

There came a time when the Fomorians and the golden-haired were at war; and in the midst of a great battle, when the Dagda's hall was not as well-guarded as usual, some of the chieftains of the Fomorians stole the great harp from the wall where it hung and fled away with it. Their wives and children and a few of their soldiers went with them, and they ran fast and far through the night until they were a long way from the battlefield. Then they thought they were safe, and turned aside into a vacant castle, sitting down to a banquet and hanging the stolen harp on the wall.

LEFT: This ancient relief probably depicts the Dagda.

ABOVE: This is said to be the harp of Brian Boru, which was originally owned by the Dagda. It is unlikely, however, to have withstood that test of time.

OPPOSITE: An artist's impression of an enchanted harp, its magical tones floating on the air.

Meanwhile, the Dagda, with two or three of his warriors, had followed hard on their track. And while they were in the midst of their banqueting, the door suddenly burst open and the Dagda stood there with his men. Some of the Fomorians sprang to their feet, but before any of them could grasp a weapon, the Dagda called out to his harp on the wall, saying, "Come to me, O my harp!"

The great harp recognized its master's voice and leapt from the wall. Whirling through the hall, sweeping aside and killing the men who got in its way, it sprang to its master's hand. And the Dagda took his harp and swept his hand across the strings in three great, solemn chords, the harp responding with the magical "Music of Tears." As the wailing harmonies smote the air, the women of the Fomorians bowed their heads and wept bitterly, the strong men turned their faces aside, and the little children sobbed their hearts out.

Again the Dagda touched the strings, and this time the magical "Music of Mirth" leapt from the harp. And when they heard it, the young Fomorian warriors began to laugh; they laughed until the cups fell from their grasp and the spears dropped from their hands, while the wine flowed from the broken bowls; they laughed until their sides ached.

Once more the Dagda touched his harp, but very, very softly. Now an air stole forth as soft as dreams and as sweet as joy: it was the magical "Music of Sleep." When they heard that, gently, gently, the Fomorian women bowed their heads in slumber; the little children crept into their mothers' laps; the old men nodded; and the young warriors drooped in their seats and closed their eyes: one after another all the Fomorians surrendered themselves to sleep.

When they were all deep in slumber, the Dagda took his harp, and he and his warriors stole softly away, returning in safety to their own homes.

THE WOOING OF ÉTAÍN

"The Wooing of Étaín" (*Tochmarc Étaíne*) is an early text of the Irish Mythological Cycle, but also features characters from the Ulster Cycle. It is partially preserved in the manuscript known as the "Book of the Dun Cow" (*Lebor na h'Uidre*), ca.1106, and is completely preserved in the *Yellow Book of Lecan* (ca.1401), written in language believed to date from the 8th or 9th century. It tells of the life and loves of Étaín, a beautiful mortal woman of the Ulaid (Ulster), and her involvement with Aengus and Midir of the Tuatha Dé Danann. The tale is told in three versions.

Version 1: The story begins when Bóann, the wife of Nechtan, conceives a child, Aengus, by her lover, the Dagda. Aengus is fostered by Midir, and when he grows to maturity takes possession from Nechtan of the Brú na Bóinne (the Palace of the Boyne – a World Heritage Site in County Meath, and the largest and one of the most important megalithic sites in Europe).

Midir visits Aengus, but is blinded by a sprig of holly thrown by boys playing in the palace. After he has been healed by the physician, Dian Cécht, Midir demands compensation from Aengus, including, among other things, the hand of the most beautiful woman in Ireland, whom he has already identified as Étaín, daughter of Ailill, king of the Ulaid. To win her for Midir, Aengus is obliged to perform various tasks for Ailill, which includes clearing plains and diverting rivers as well as handing over Étaín's weight in gold and silver. Midir takes Étaín as his wife.

But Midir's first wife, Fúamnach, sick with jealousy, turns Étaín into a pool of water, out of which, as it evaporates, emerges a beautiful purple fly. Midir knows the fly is Étaín, and she accompanies him wherever he goes. But Fúamnach conjures up a storm which blows the fly away, and Étaín drifts for seven years before landing on Aengus' clothing, exhausted. Aengus makes her a crystal bower which he carries around with him until she returns to health. Fuamnach conjures up

another storm and blows Étaín away from Aengus, and after another seven years Étaín lands in a golden cup in the hand of the wife of Étar, a warrior of the Ulaid in the time of Conchobar mac Nessa. Étar's wife drinks from the cup, swallows the fly, and becomes pregnant. Étaín is reborn 1,002 years after her first birth. Meanwhile, Aengus hunts down Fúamnach and cuts off her head.

Version 2: The High King of Ireland, Eochu Airem, seeks a wife because the local rulers refuse to submit to a king who has no queen. He sends messengers to find the most beautiful woman in Ireland, and they find Étaín. Eochu falls in love with Étaín and marries her, but his brother, Ailill, also falls for her, and is tortured by unrequited love.

Eochu departs from Tara on a tour of Ireland, leaving Étaín with the dying Ailill, who tells her the cause of his sickness, which he says would be cured if she gave the word. She tells him she wants him to be well, and he begins to get better but says that the cure will only be complete if she agrees to meet him on the hill above the house, so as not to shame the king in his own house. She agrees to do so three

ABOVE: Tara, the seat of the High Kings of Ireland.

OPPOSITE: The Iron Age Corlea Trackway is evocative of Midir's causeway that crossed the bog of Móin Lámrige.

18

times, but each time she goes to meet Ailill, she in fact meets Midir, who has put Ailill to sleep and assumed his appearance. On the third occasion Midir reveals his identity, telling Étaín who he really is. She finally agrees to go with him, but only if Eochu agrees to let her go.

Version 3: Later, after Ailill has fully recovered and Eochu has returned home, Midir comes to Tara and challenges Eochu to play fidchell, an ancient Irish board game with him. They play for ever-increasing stakes, which Eochu keeps winning and Midir has to pay up. One such game compels Midir to build a causeway across the bog of Móin Lámrige (the Corlea Trackway, an Iron Age wooden causeway, built across a bog in County Longford, is a real-life counterpart to this legendary road). Finally, Midir suggests they play for a kiss and an embrace from Étaín, and this time he wins. Eochu tells Midir to come back in a year for his winnings and gathers his best warriors at Tara to prepare for the return. Despite the heavy guard, Midir appears inside the house. Eochu agrees that Midir may embrace Étaín, but when he does, the pair fly away through the skylight, turning into swans as they do so.

Eochu instructs his men to dig up every fairy mound (*síd*) in Ireland until his wife is returned to him. Finally, when they begin to dig at Midir's *síd* at Brí Léith, Midir appears and promises to give Étaín back. But at the appointed time, Midir brings 50 women, who all look alike, and tells Eochu to pick the one he thinks is Étaín. Eochu chooses the woman he thinks is his wife, takes her home and sleeps with her. She becomes pregnant and bears him a daughter.

Later, Midir appears and tells Eochu that Étaín had been pregnant when he took her, and that the woman Eochu had chosen was his own daughter, who had been born in Midir's *síd*. Out of shame, Eochu orders the daughter of this incestuous union to be exposed, but she is found and brought up by a herdsman and his wife. She later marries Eochu's successor, Eterscél, becoming the mother of the High King Conaire Mór (she is called Mess Búachalla and is the daughter of Étaín and Eochu).

The story ends with Eochu's death at the hands of Sigmall Cael, Midir's grandson. (Somewhat confusingly, in the "Destruction of Da Derga's Hostel," *Togail Bruidne Dá Derga*, an Irish tale of the Ulster Cycle, Mess Búachalla is the daughter of Eochu's brother, Eochu Feidlech, and of Étaín.)

THE DREAM OF AENGUS

Aengus' first glimpse of his future wife, Caer, was in a dream and, on waking, he realized that he was desperately in love. He told his mother Bóann of his dream, and she set out to search the whole of Ireland for the girl. After a year had passed, and Bóann had still not found the girl, the Dagda was called and he too searched for a whole year but failed to find her. Eventually, Bodhb Dearg (Bov the Red), the Dagda's aide, was called and finally, after another year, Caer was found.

Aengus was taken to a lake where 150 maidens were paired up and chained with gold. He spotted his love immediately and learned that her name was Caer and that she was the daughter of Ethal and Anubal. On November 1 (the Celtic

festival of Samhain), Caer, and the other maidens, were transformed into swans for one year, and Aengus was told that if he could correctly identify her from among the others he could marry her.

A year from that day he went out to the lake and called to her, and when he found her he turned into a swan himself. Aengus and Caer flew off together, singing a beautiful song, and all who heard them fell asleep for three days and three nights.

Aengus is a member of the Tuatha Dé Danann and a god of love, beauty, youth and poetic inspiration; some tales tell how he even had the power to breathe life back into the dead.

BELOW: Aengus and Caer turned into beautiful swans.

CATH MAIGE TUIREADH

The Tuatha Dé Danann had defeated the Fir Bolg (one of the races that inhabited the island of Ireland prior to the arrival of the Tuatha Dé Danann) at the first Battle of Maige Tuireadh and driven them to the West of Ireland, but they did not enjoy precedence for long. Soon they were forced to do battle with the Fomorians, adepts of the magic arts who lived in the westernmost islands.

During the first battle, Nuada the king had lost his arm and so, according to ancient custom, he was obliged to stand down as ruler as defects were not permitted in sovereigns. Bres (the Beautiful), whose father Elatha was a king of the Fomorians, but who had been raised among his mother's kin, the Tuatha Dé Danann, was chosen in his stead. The rule of Bres, however, soon became oppressive, for he was an unpopular king who favored his Fomorian kin above the Tuatha Dé Danann. Bres, moreover, was missing the most important characteristic of every true king, namely a generous spirit.

The chieftains of the Tuatha Dé Danann complained that "their knives were not greased by him and however often they visited him their breaths did not smell of ale." There was no entertainment for them in the royal household, no poets, musicians, acrobats or buffoons. In the end retribution was hastened by a poet's verses.

When Coirbre, the poet of the Tuatha Dé Danann, was received by Bres with scant hospitality, he retaliated with magic-tipped satire (the first that was made in Ireland), and nothing but decay was on Bres from that hour. The chieftains of the Tuatha Dé Danann demanded he renounce his kingship, so he went out to muster an army of the Fomorians to support him.

In the meantime, Nuada had been fitted with a silver arm by the physician, Dían Cécht, and was reinstated in the sovereignty; from that time forward he was known as Nuada Airgetlám (of the Silver Arm). Then Lugh the Long-Handed arrived on the scene and, as soon as Nuada had received proof of his technical abilities, he

relinquished the throne to Lugh in the hope that he would lead the Tuatha Dé Danann to victory against the Fomorians.

Under Lugh's leadership, preparations were soon underway and each of the craftsmen and magicians of the Tuatha Dé Danann promised their own special contributions. The craftsmen fashioned wondrous weapons; the sorcerers hurled the mountains of Ireland onto the Fomorians; the cupbearers concealed from them the waters of Ireland's lakes and streams; the Druids cast down on them showers of fire, and deprived them of two-thirds of their strength and courage, binding in their bodies the urine of men and horses.

There was great slaughter on both sides, once the battle had been joined in earnest. The slain of the Fomorians remained so, but those of the Tuatha Dé Danann were cast into a well over which Dian Cécht and his three children sang spells, and by their magic restored them to life. Lugh also used his powers, moving around his army on one foot and with one eye, while chanting an incantation to lend them strength and courage. He thus assumed the traditional posture of the sorcerer and one which was attributed to the Fomorians.

He then had to face the dreaded Balor of the Evil Eye. Balor's eye was such that he needed four men to raise its lid and when uncovered its venomous gaze could disable an army. As soon as Lugh saw the eye open against him he cast a slingshot which drove it through to the back of Balor's head so that it wrought destruction on his own followers.

The Fomorians were routed and expelled forever from Ireland. Bres was captured and sought to save his own life by promising first that the cattle in Ireland should always be in milk, and secondly, that there should be a harvest in every quarter of the year. Both offers were rejected but he was finally spared in return for advice on the proper times for ploughing, sowing and reaping. With that, the Tuatha Dé Danann prospered in Ireland for many years to come and never lacked for anything.

THE CHILDREN OF LIR

Lough Derravaragh is associated with one of the most famous tales of Irish imaginative literature: "The Fate of the Children of Lir" (*Oidhe Chlann Lir*). Founded partly on fact and partly on fiction, the tale is classed as belonging to what are generally known as "The Three Sorrows of Storytelling" (*Tri Truagha na Scealaidheachta*), the other two being "The Exile of the Sons of Uisneach" and "The Faith of the Children of Tuireann."

Lir was a chieftain of the Tuatha Dé Danann tribe. On the death of the Dagda, their king, a convention of chiefs elected the Dagda's son, Bodhb Dearg, to succeed him, a decision that offended Lir, who felt he had a greater claim to the kingship.

Shortly after, Lir's wife died and Bodhb Dearg, who had three beautiful foster-daughters, in a gesture of friendship, offered Lir the choice of one of them as his wife. Lir chose Aobh (Eve), the

eldest, who bore him four beautiful children: Fionnuala, Aodh, Fiachra and Conn. Tragedy struck, however, and Aobh died. Lir was heartbroken and he too would have died but for the great love he bore for his children. After a time, Bodhb Dearg offered Lir Aoife, the sister of Aobh, as wife, and accordingly Lir and Aoife were married.

Lir's four children were famous for their beauty and were beloved by all the Tuatha Dé Danann. At first, Aoife cared for the children as if she were their real mother, but evil touched her heart and she grew insanely jealous of Lir's devotion to his children.

One morning, when Lir was away hunting, Aoife took the children out in her chariot to visit their grandfather, Bodhb Dearg. Stopping at Lough Derravaragh, she led the children to the water to let them bathe, but as soon as they were in the lake she used her magic wand to change them into four beautiful swans, cursing them to spend 300 years on Lough Derravaragh, 300 years on the Sea of Moyle (North Channel) and 300 years on the Bay of Erris, County Mayo.

OPPOSITE: A sculpture of the Children of Lir in Dublin's Garden of Remembrance.

Aoife allowed the children to retain their speech and also gave them the power to sing in a way surpassing all earthly beings. Legend has it that Bodhb Dearg punished Aoife for this crime by transforming her into a demon of the air.

Throughout their 300 years on Lough Derravaragh, great crowds frequently gathered to listen to the singing of the swans, but later, on the Sea of Moyle and finally on the Bay of Erris, the four swan-children underwent great sufferings.

THE FOUR CYCLES OF IRISH MYTHOLOGY

During their final days on the Bay of Erris, the children learn of a holy man called Patrick, who had come to Ireland to tell the people about the Christian faith. As one of Patrick's disciples prayed with them their feathers fell away and they were restored to their human form, although they were now three feeble old men and an old woman. Patrick's disciple, St. Caemhoch, baptized them before they died, and they were buried together in the one grave as they had wished.

LEFT: Lir and the Swans, *from the drawing by J. H. Bacon, A.R.A.*

OPPOSITE: The Straits of Moyle or Sea of Moyle is the name given to the narrowest expanse of sea in the North Channel between northeastern Ireland (County Antrim) and southwestern Scotland (Mull of Kintyre).

BELOW: Lough Derravaragh in County Westmeath.

THE ULSTER CYCLE

The stories of the Ulster Cycle are set in and around the reign of King Conchobar mac Nessa, who ruled the Ulaid from Emain Macha (now Navan Fort near Armagh). The most important hero of the cycle is Conchobar's nephew, Cú Chulainn. The Ulaid are most often in conflict with the Connachta, led by their queen, Medb (Maeve), her husband, Ailill, and their ally Fergus mac Róich, a former king of the Ulaid in exile. The longest and

RIGHT: Queen Maeve and the Druid, by Stephen Reid.

BELOW: Emain Macha (Navan Fort), the seat of the kings of the Ulaid (Ulster).

OPPOSITE: One of the earliest Neolithic passage tombs in the Carrowmore complex, the Knocknarea cairn can be clearly seen high up in the background. It is known as Queen Medb's (Maeve's) tomb.

most important story of the cycle is the "Cattle Raid of Cooley" (*Táin Bó Cúailnge*), in which Medb raises an enormous army to invade the Cooley peninsula and steal the Ulaid's prize bull, Donn Cúailnge, opposed only by the 17-year-old Cú Chulainn. Cú Chulainn, in particular, has superhuman fighting skills, the result of his semi-divine ancestry, and when particularly aroused his battle-contortion (*ríastrad*) transforms him into an unrecognizable monster who knows neither friend nor foe.

Perhaps the best-known story of the Ulster Cycle is "Deirdre of the Sorrows," while others tell of the births, courtships and deaths of the characters and of the conflicts arising between them.

DEIRDRE OF THE SORROWS

Deirdre was the daughter of the royal storyteller, Fedlimid mac Daill. Before she was born, Cathbad, the chief Druid at the court of Conchobar mac Nessa, King of Ulster, prophesied that Fedlimid's daughter would grow up to be a great beauty, and that kings and lords would go to war over her; much blood would be shed, and Ulster's three greatest warriors would be forced into exile for her sake. Many, therefore, urged Fedlimid to kill the baby at birth, but Conchobar, tempted by this promise of beauty, and with the plan forming in his mind of marrying Deirdre when she was old enough, decided to keep the child for himself, raising her in seclusion with the help of Leabharcham, an old woman.

Deirdre grew up, and told Leabharcham that the only man she could ever love would have hair the color of the raven, skin as white as snow, and lips as red as blood. Now Leabharcham knew of such a man called Naoise, a hunter and singer at Conchobar's court. With the collusion of Leabharcham, Deirdre met Naoise who, knowing she was destined for the king, tried at first to avoid her, but Deirdre persuaded him into eloping with her. Accompanied by his fiercely loyal brothers, Ardan and Ainnle, the Sons of Uisnech, the two fled to Loch Etive in Scotland, where they lived an idyllic life which was to be short-lived, for the furious, humiliated Conchobar had managed to track them down.

Conchobar sent Fergus mac Róich with an invitation to the couple to return and Fergus' own promise of a safe conduct home, but on the way back to Emain Macha, Fergus, this being part of the king's plan, was forced by his personal *geis* (a sacred obligation or prohibition, similar to being under a vow or spell) to accept an invitation to a feast. Fergus sent Deirdre and the Sons of Uisnech on to Emain Macha with his son to protect them. After

they had arrived, Conchobar sent Leabharcham to spy on Deirdre to see if she had retained her beauty. Leabharcham, in an effort to protect Deirdre, told the king that Deirdre had lost her beauty, but Conchobar, being mistrustful, sent another spy, Gelbann, who was able to catch a glimpse of Deirdre but was seen by Naoise, who threw a gold chess piece at Gelbann and put out his eye. Gelbann was able to get back to Conchobar, however, and to tell him that Deirdre was as beautiful as ever.

Conchobar called on his warriors to attack the Red Branch House where Deirdre and the Sons of Uisnech were lodging. Naoise and his brothers fought valiantly, helped by a few Red Branch warriors, before Conchobar evoked their oath of loyalty to him and had Deirdre dragged to his side. At this point, Éogan mac Durthacht threw a spear, killing Naoise, and his brothers lost their lives shortly afterwards.

After the death of Naoise, Conchobar took Deirdre as his wife. After a year, angered by Deirdre's continuing coldness, Conchobar asked her to name the person in the world whom she hated most, besides himself. She answered, "Éogan mac Durthacht," the man who had murdered Naoise, to which Conchobar declared that he would give her to Éogan. As she was being taken to Éogan, Conchobar taunted her further, saying she resembled a ewe between two rams. At this, Deirdre threw herself from the chariot, dashing her head to pieces against a rock. In other versions of the story, she dies of grief.

ABOVE: Deirdre's Lament, by J. H. Bacon.

LEFT: Deirdre, Naoise and his loyal brothers shared a short-lived though idyllic life on the shores of the beautiful Loch Etive in Scotland.

THE CATTLE RAID OF COOLEY

"The Cattle Raid of Cooley" (*Táin bó Cúailnge*) is an Old Irish epic-like tale that is the longest of the Ulster Cycle of heroic tales and deals with the conflict between the Ulaid (Ulster) and Connacht (Connaught) over possession of the brown bull of Cooley. The tale was composed in prose with verse passages in the 7th and 8th centuries. It is partially preserved in the "Book of the Dun Cow" (ca. 1100) and is also to be found in *The Book of Leinster* (ca. 1160) and *The Yellow Book of Lecan* (late 14th century). Although it contains passages of lively narrative and witty dialogue, it is not a coherent work of art, and its text has been marred by revisions and interpolations. It is of particular value to the literary historian in that the reworkings provide a record of the degeneration of the Irish style; for example, the bare prose of

ABOVE: A page from the original "Book of the Dun Cow," which tells the tale of "The Cattle Raid of Cooley."

the earlier passages is later replaced by bombast and alliteration, and ruthless humor quickly degenerates into sentimentality.

The tale's plot is as follows. Medb, the warrior queen of Connacht, enters into a dispute with her husband, Ailill, over their respective wealth. Because possession of the white-horned bull guarantees Ailill's superiority, Medb resolves to secure the even-more-famous brown bull of Cooley from the Ulstermen. Although Medb is warned of impending doom by a prophetess, the Connacht army proceeds to Ulster. The Ulster warriors are temporarily disabled by a curse, but Cú Chulainn, the youthful Ulster champion, is exempt from the curse and single-handedly holds off the Connachtmen. The climax of the fighting is a three-day combat between Cú Chulainn and Fer Díad, his friend and foster-brother, who is in exile and fighting with the Connacht forces. Cú Chulainn is victorious and, nearly dead from wounds and exhaustion, is joined by the Ulster army, which routs the enemy. The brown bull, however, has been captured by Connacht and defeats Ailill's white-horned bull, after which peace is made.

Cú Chulainn is both helped and hindered by supernatural figures. Before one combat the Morrigan, the goddess of battle, visits him in the form of a beautiful young woman and offers him her love, but he spurns her. She then threatens to interfere in his next fight, which she does, first in the form of an eel which trips him in the ford, then as a wolf which stampedes cattle across the ford, and finally as a heifer at the head of the stampede, but in each form Cú Chulainn wounds her. After he defeats his opponent, the Morrigan appears to him in the form of an old woman milking a cow, with wounds corresponding to the ones Cú Chulainn gave her in her animal forms. She offers him three drinks of milk. With each drink he blesses her, and the blessings heal her wounds.

Undoubtedly the finest section is that in which Fergus mac Róich, an exile from Ulster at the Connacht court, recalls for Medb and Ailill the heroic deeds of Cú Chulainn's youth.

THE FOUR CYCLES OF IRISH MYTHOLOGY

THE FENIAN CYCLE

The Fenian Cycle, otherwise known as the Finn Cycle or Finnian Tales, is also referred to as the Ossianic Cycle after Oisín, the son of Fionn mac Cumhaill and of Sadhb, the daughter of Bodb Dearg. Much of the cycle (or *Fiannaidheacht*), a body of prose and verse recalling the exploits of the mythical hero Fionn mac Cumhaill (Finn McCool) and of his warriors, the Fianna Éireann, is purported to have been narrated by Oisín, regarded as the legendary poet of Ireland and himself a Fianna warrior. The cycle also tells the stories of other Fianna members, such as Caílte, Diarmuid, Oisín's son Oscar, and Fionn's enemy, Goll mac Morna. Tales of Fionn mac Cumhaill also occur in the mythologies of Scotland and of the Isle of Man.

Fionn mac Cumhaill is also said to have created the Giant's Causeway, an area of about 40,000 interlocking basalt columns, the result of an ancient volcanic eruption in County Antrim on the northeastern coast of Ireland. He is said to have built the Giant's Causeway as stepping-stones to

Scotland, so as not to get his feet wet; he also once scooped up part of Ireland to fling it at a rival, but missed and fragments landed in the Irish Sea, some becoming the Isle of Man, Rockall, and the void that was created becoming Lough Neagh. Fingal's Cave, in the Outer Hebrides, Scotland, is also said to be named after Fionn, and this and the Giant's Causeway are the most famous sites of basalt columns in Britain and maybe the whole world.

LEFT: Fingal's Cave in the Outer Hebrides.

ABOVE: Fionn mac Cumhaill Comes to the Aid of the Fianna, by Stephen Reid.

OPPOSITE: In legend, the Giant's Causeway in County Antrim is said to have been created by the giant Fionn mac Cumhaill.

THE SALMON OF WISDOM

In Irish myth, nine hazel trees of wisdom surrounded the sacred Well of Knowledge, in which an ancient salmon lived, which fed on the hazelnuts as they fell into the pool. Nearby lived an old poet, Finn Eces, who greatly desired to catch the salmon and make a fine meal of it, because he had heard that anyone eating that wise fish would gain all the knowledge in the world.

As a youth, Fionn mac Cumhaill came to the poet's house as his apprentice. One day, the poet finally caught the salmon, and he instructed Fionn to cook it for him. But as Fionn was doing so, he accidentally burned his thumb on the fish's flank. He sucked his thumb to ease the pain, and as a result tasted the salmon before his master; thus Fionn was the one to gain the wisdom of the salmon and the gift of prophecy. After that, whenever Fionn needed some special knowledge, he would suck his thumb and all would be revealed.

Like many of the magical beasts of Irish folklore, the fish is renewed to be eaten again and

BELOW & OPPOSITE: Hazelnut-eating salmon appear in many Irish stories.

again. This metaphor for the gaining of wisdom speaks of visiting the quiet places within ourselves (the quiet pool), patiently feeding on the morsels of knowledge (the hazelnuts), patiently seeking understanding (the salmon), and distilling it into the wisdom and inspiration needed to create (poetry). In Welsh mythology, the story of how the poet Taliesin received his wisdom follows a similar pattern.

FIONN MAC CUMHAIL AND THE GIANT CUHULLIN

Fionn mac Cumhaill is sometimes portrayed as a magical, benevolent giant, and the most famous story attached to Fionn in this guise tells of how, one day, while sucking his magic thumb (which allows him to see everything that is going on anywhere), Fionn sees that the giant Cuhullin is coming to fight him. Knowing he can never

withstand Cuhullin, Fionn asks his wife Oona to help him. So she dresses her husband as a baby and he hides in a cradle; then she makes a batch of griddle-cakes, hiding griddle-irons in some of them. When Cuhullin arrives, Oona tells him that Fionn is out but will shortly return. As Cuhullin waits for Fionn, he tries to intimidate Oona with his immense power, breaking rocks with his middle finger. Oona then offers Cuhullin a griddle-cake with a griddle-iron hidden in it, but on biting into it the iron chips his teeth. Oona scolds him for being weak (saying her husband had no trouble at all eating such cakes), and feeds one without an iron in it to Fionn. Cuhullin is so amazed at the strength of the baby's teeth that, at Oona's prompting, he puts his fingers in Fionn's mouth to feel how sharp the teeth are. Fionn bites off Cuhullin's middle finger and, having lost the source of his power, Cuhullin shrinks to the size of an ordinary mortal and runs away in shame.

THE FIANNA ÉIREANN (THE FENIAN KNIGHTS)

There is a fort near the Killeries in Connemara known as Lis-na-Keeran. One day the powerful chief, who inhabited the fort, invited the great Fionn mac Cumhaill, with his son Oscar and a band of Fenian knights, to a great banquet. But when the guests arrived they found no chairs set out for them, only rough benches of wood placed around the table.

Oscar and his father, suspecting treachery, refrained from taking their places and stood watching instead. The knights, however, fearing nothing, sat down to the feast but were instantly fixed to their benches by magic so that they could neither rise nor move.

Then Fionn began to suck his thumb, from which he always derived knowledge of the future, and by his magic power saw clearly a great and terrible warrior riding purposefully toward the fort. Fionn knew immediately that, unless the warrior could be stopped before crossing a certain ford, they must all die, for they had been brought to Lis-na-Keeran only to be slain. Unless the warrior was killed, and his blood sprinkled on the Fenian knights, Fionn also knew that they must remain fixed to the wooden benches forever.

So Oscar of the Lionheart rushed forth to the encounter and, flinging his spear at the mighty horseman, fought with him desperately until sunset. At last Oscar triumphed; victory was his and he cut off the head of his adversary. He carried the

bleeding head on his spear to the fort, where he let the blood fall upon the Fenian knights who were transfixed by magic. At this, they all sprang up but for one, on whom, unhappily, no blood had fallen. As the knight remained fixed to the bench, his companions attempted to rescue him, but when they attempted to remove him by force, the skin of his thighs was left stuck to the bench. The knight seemed likely to die, and so the others killed a sheep, and, wrapping the fleece around the knight, hoped that the warmth from the animal would be transferred to his body. Thus the knight was cured, but ever after, strange to tell, 98 lbs of wool were annually shorn from his body for as long as he lived.

This tale is set in the rugged but beautiful Connemara countryside.

THE PURSUIT OF DIARMUID AND GRÁINNE

This tale, from the Fenian Cycle, concerns a love triangle between the great warrior Fionn mac Cumhaill, the beautiful Princess Gráinne, and her paramour Diarmuid Ua Duibhne. Surviving texts are in modern Irish, the earliest dating from the 16th century, but some elements of the material go back as far as the 10th century AD.

The story begins with the aging Fionn, leader of the Fianna, grieving over the death of his wife, Maigneis. His men find that Gráinne, the daughter of High King Cormac mac Airt, is the worthiest of all women, and arrangements are made for their wedding. At their betrothal feast, however, Gráinne is distressed to find that Fionn is older than her own father, and becomes enamored by Fionn's handsome warrior Diarmuid (according to some versions, this is because of the magical "love spot" on Diarmuid's forehead that makes him irresistible). She slips a sleeping potion to the rest of the guests and encourages Diarmuid to run away with her. At first he refuses but, out of loyalty to Fionn, relents when Gráinne threatens him with a *geis*, forcing him to comply. They hide in a forest near the River Shannon, and Fionn sets off in hot pursuit. The pair evade him several times with the help of other Fianna members and Aengus, Diarmuid's foster-father, wraps Gráinne in his cloak of invisibility while Diarmuid leaps over the pursuers' heads.

Variants of the tale, from Ireland and Scotland, contain different episodes, sending Diarmuid and Gráinne to all manner of places. Commonly, Diarmuid at first refuses to sleep with Gráinne out of respect for Fionn; in one version she teases Diarmuid that the water that has splashed up her leg is more adventurous than he is (a similar quip appears in some versions of the Tristan and Isolde legend). Another episode describes how the newly pregnant Gráinne develops a craving for the rowanberries guarded by the one-eyed giant, Searbhán; though at first friendly toward the lovers, Searbhán angrily refuses to give up the berries and Diarmuid is obliged to fight him for them. Searbhán's magic protects him from Diarmuid's weapons, but Diarmuid eventually triumphs by turning the giant's own iron club against him.

After many such adventures, Diarmuid's foster-father, Aengus, negotiates peace with Fionn. The lovers settle in Keshcorran, County Sligo, where they have five children; in other versions, Fionn marries Gráinne's sister. Eventually, Fionn

organizes a boar hunt near Benbulbin and Diarmuid joins in, in spite of a prediction that he will be killed by a boar. Indeed, the creature wounds him mortally at the same time as he deals it a fatal blow. Fionn has the power to heal his dying comrade by simply letting him drink water from his hands, but he lets the water slip through his fingers twice. Finally Fionn's grandson, Oscar, threatens him with violence if he does not help Diarmuid, but when he returns from the well on the third attempt it is too late. Diarmuid has died.

Versions differ as to Gráinne's subsequent actions. In some, Aengus takes Diarmuid's body to his home at Brú na Bóinne. In others, Gráinne swears her children to avenge their father's death upon Fionn, while in still others she grieves until she herself dies. Sometimes she is reconciled with Fionn and negotiates peace between him and her sons, or goes as far, in the end, as to marry Fionn at last.

ABOVE: Rowanberries feature in the tale of Diarmuid and Gráinne.

BELOW: The River Shannon, in the vicinity of which Gráinne and Diarmuid hide from Fionn mac Cumhaill.

THE HISTORICAL CYCLE

During the medieval period in Ireland, it was the custom for professional poets (bards) to record the history of the family or king in whose service they were employed. This they did in poems that blended the mythological and symbolic and the historical to a greater or lesser degree. The resulting stories form what has come to be known as the Historical or King Cycle, or more correctly Cycles, in that there were a number of independent groupings.

Tara, a hill located in County Meath, was the center of ancient Ireland and the seat of the kings from the earliest times until the 6th century. The Tatra Feis was held every three years at Samhain, when a new king was chosen by the Druids, after which they killed and ate a white bull. The chief Druid would dream about the future king and upon wakening make his decision based on his dream.

The Historical Cycle includes stories of the legendary kings of Ireland, of Cormac mac Airt, Niall of the Nine Hostages, Éogan Mór, Conall Corc, Guaire Aidne mac Colmáin, Diarmait mac Cerbaill, Lugaid mac Con, Conn of the Hundred Battles, Lóegaire mac Néill, Crimthann mac Fidaig and Brian Boru. But the greatest glory of the cycle is "The Frenzy of Sweeney" (*Buile Suibhne*), a 12th-century tale told in a mixture of verse and prose.

RIGHT: The Rock of Cashel was the traditional seat of the kings of Munster for several hundred years prior to the Norman invasion, the most famous of them being Brian Boru who, for a brief, shining moment, became king of a unified Celtic Ireland, having ended the Viking hold over large parts of the country. In 978 Brian Boru was crowned here as the first non-Eóghanacht king of Cashel and Munster in over 500 years. In 1101 his great-grandson, King Muircheartach Ua Briain, gave the place to the bishop of Limerick, which also denied it forever to the MacCarthys, the senior branch of the Eóganachta, an Irish dynasty centered around Cashel which had dominated southern Ireland from around the 7th century AD.

THE FRENZY OF SWEENEY (BUILE SUIBHNE)

Sweeney (Suibhne), king of Dalriada, was greatly annoyed by the sound of a bell ringing, and discovering that it came from Bishop Ronan Finn's church, the pagan king stormed naked into the church, dragged the bishop out, and threw his psalter into a lake. He would have killed the bishop but for the fact that he was called away to fight the Battle of Mag Rath. Prior to the battle, Bishop Ronan had blessed the troops, but Sweeney had taken the sprinkling of holy water as a taunt and killed one of the bishop's psalmists with a spear and thrown another spear at Ronan himself. The spear struck Ronan's bell and broke it, at which Ronan cursed Sweeney with madness. His curse was that,

as the sound of the bell had been broken, so now would any other such sound make Sweeney go mad, and that, as Sweeney had killed one of Ronan's monks, so too would Sweeney die at spear point. When the battle began, Sweeney sunk into insanity and, dropping his weapon, began to levitate like a bird.

From this point on, Sweeney hopped, birdlike, from spot to spot. Also, like a bird, he was loath to trust human beings. His kinsmen and subjects filled him with fear, causing him to flee from place to place, living naked and hungry. After seven years in the wild, Sweeney's reason was briefly restored with the help of his kinsmen, who very gently coaxed him back to reason; while recuperating, however, an old hag taunted him into partaking in a

contest of leaping. As Sweeney leapt along after the hag, he again took flight and returned to madness. Eventually, after travels throughout Ireland and western England, Sweeney was given shelter by Bishop Moling, with whom he lived, broken and old, entrusted to the care of a parish woman. The woman's husband, a herder, however, grew jealous and attacked Sweeney with a spear. On his death, Sweeney received the sacrament and died in in a state of grace.

Many poets, most notably T. S. Eliot and Seamus Heaney, have been influenced by the story, with Heaney publishing a translation of the work into English, which he entitled "Sweeney Astray." The author Flann O'Brien also incorporated much of the story of Buile Suibhne into his comic novel,

At Swim-Two-Birds, while another version from the Irish text, entitled "The Poems of Sweeney Peregrine," was published by the Irish poet Trevor Joyce. Sweeney also appears as a character in Neil Gaiman's novel, *American Gods*, and a contemporary version of the legend, by the poet Patricia Monaghan, explores Sweeney as an archetype of the warrior suffering from "Soldier's Heart."

King Sweeney spent many years living with his madness and wandering in the wild Irish countryside.

CHAPTER TWO
IRISH SAINTS

ST. PATRICK

St. Patrick was a Roman-British, Christian missionary, who is the most generally recognized patron saint of Ireland or Apostle of Ireland, although Brigid of Kildare and Columba are also acknowledged in this role. The dates of Patrick's life cannot be fixed with certainty, but he was active as a missionary in Ireland during the second half of the fifth century AD.

Patrick was born in Britain to wealthy parents near to the end of the 4th century, and is believed to have died on March 17 in around 460. Although his father, Calpurnius, was a Christian deacon, he probably assumed the role because of tax incentives and there is no evidence that Patrick came from a particularly religious family. When he was about 16,

Patrick was captured by pirates who carried him off as a slave to Ireland, where he worked as a herdsman, remaining a captive there for six years. He writes that his faith grew in captivity, and that he prayed daily. After six years he heard voices telling him he would soon go home, and then that his ship was ready. Fleeing his master, he walked to a port, 200 miles away, where he found a ship and, after various adventures, returned home to his family, now in his early 20s.

After escaping back to Britain, Patrick received a second revelation in which an angel tells him to return to Ireland as a missionary. Soon after, Patrick began to train for the priesthood, a course of study that lasted more than 15 years. After his ordination as a priest, he was sent to Ireland with a

dual mission: to minister to Christians already living in Ireland and to begin to convert the Irish, although this contradicts the widely held notion that Patrick introduced Christianity to Ireland.

Although there were a small number of Christians in Ireland, most of the Irish Celts were pagans, following a nature-based religion. Patrick, being already familiar with the Irish language and culture, sensibly chose to incorporate these pre-existing beliefs into his Christian mission rather than attempting to eradicate them; he used bonfires to celebrate Easter, since the Irish honored their gods with fire, and superimposed the Christian cross on top of the powerful pagan sun symbol to create a Celtic cross, making it easier and more natural for the Irish to absorb the new religion.

Where Patrick was buried is a mystery. Among other places, a chapel to St. Patrick at Glastonbury, in Somerset, England, claims to be his tomb, while a shrine in County Down, Ireland, is said to possess the jawbone of the saint, which is used to alleviate the pain of childbirth, prevent epileptic fits, and avert the evil eye.

THE SHAMROCK

Perhaps the best-known legend of St. Patrick involves the shamrock, the little plant that is famous throughout the world as the national emblem of Ireland. After training as a priest, then becoming a bishop, Patrick arrived in Ireland in AD 432 and immediately set about trying to covert the pagan Celts who inhabited the island.

Having previously lived and worked there, during his period of slavery in Ireland, he would have been well aware that the number three held special significance in Celtic tradition (and, indeed, in many pagan beliefs), and he applied this knowledge in a clever way.

He used the shamrock, a three-leaved clover that grows all over the island, to explain the Christian concept of the Holy Trinity, i.e., the theory that God the Father, God the Son and God the Holy Spirit are separate elements of a single entity.

OPPOSITE: St. Patrick's grave site in the grounds of Down Cathedral, Downpatrick.

ABOVE: The statue of St. Patrick on Croagh Patrick, an important site of pilgrimage in County Mayo.

IRISH SAINTS

ST. PATRICK'S BREASTPLATE

This is a hymn of hope attributed to St. Patrick,
known as "St. Patrick's Breastplate" or "The Deer's
Cry." It is said to have been written while the saint,
on his way to the Hill of Tara in the Boyne Valley
(the site of the ancient capital of Ireland and, to the
Druids, the sacred dwelling place of their gods),
was preparing himself to confront and convert the
High King of Ireland Lóegaire mac Néill, and his
subjects, to Christianity. Patrick is said to have used
a magic mist (*féth fíada*), which the Tuatha Dé
Danann once used to enshroud themselves,
rendering their presence invisible to the human
eye, to transform himself and his companion into
wild deer to escape ambush and capture.

I bind unto myself today
The strong Name of the Trinity,
By invocation of the same
The Three in One and One in Three.

I bind this today to me forever
By power of faith, Christ's incarnation;
His baptism in Jordan river,
His death on Cross for my salvation;
His bursting from the spicèd tomb,
His riding up the heavenly way,
His coming at the day of doom
I bind unto myself today.

I bind unto myself the power
Of the great love of cherubim;

IRELAND: LEGENDS & FOLKLORE

The sweet "Well done" in judgment hour,
The service of the seraphim,
Confessors' faith, Apostles' word,
The Patriarchs' prayers, the prophets' scrolls,
All good deeds done unto the Lord
And purity of virgin souls.

I bind unto myself today
The virtues of the star-lit heaven,
The glorious sun's life-giving ray,
The whiteness of the moon at even,
The flashing of the lightning free,
The whirling wind's tempestuous shocks,
The stable earth, the deep salt sea
Around the old eternal rocks.

I bind unto myself today
The power of God to hold and lead,
His eye to watch, His might to stay,
His ear to hearken to my need.
The wisdom of my God to teach,
His hand to guide, His shield to ward;
The word of God to give me speech,
His heavenly host to be my guard.

Against the demon snares of sin,
The vice that gives temptation force,
The natural lusts that war within,
The hostile men that mar my course;
Or few or many, far or nigh,

In every place and in all hours,
Against their fierce hostility
I bind to me these holy powers.

Against all Satan's spells and wiles,
Against false words of heresy,
Against the knowledge that defiles,
Against the heart's idolatry,
Against the wizard's evil craft,
Against the death wound and the burning,
The choking wave, the poisoned shaft,
Protect me, Christ, till Thy returning.

Christ be with me, Christ within me,
Christ behind me, Christ before me,
Christ beside me, Christ to win me,
Christ to comfort and restore me.
Christ beneath me, Christ above me,
Christ in quiet, Christ in danger,
Christ in hearts of all that love me,
Christ in mouth of friend and stranger.

I bind unto myself the Name,
The strong Name of the Trinity,
By invocation of the same,
The Three in One and One in Three.
By Whom all nature hath creation,
Eternal Father, Spirit, Word
Praise to the Lord of my salvation,
Salvation is of Christ the Lord.

THE MAGIC FIRE

Beltane is an ancient Celtic festival celebrated in
Ireland, Scotland and the Isle of Man. It is a ritual
fire festival held to guarantee the fertility of crops
and animals in the coming year. It marks the
beginning of summer and has links with similar
festivals held elsewhere in Europe, such as the
Welsh Calan Mai and the German Walpurgisnacht.
Beltane is a cross-quarter day, which marks the
midpoint in the sun's progress between the spring
equinox and summer solstice. Although Beltane is
synonymous with May Day, the astronomical date
for this midpoint is nearer to May 5 or 7, but this
can vary from year to year.

Beltane regained popularity during the Celtic
Revival and is still observed as a cultural festival by
some. Today, Beltane is also observed as a religious
festival by Celtic neopagans, while Wiccans adopted
the name Beltane for their May festival.

The Celtic Beltane (Feast of the Fires) was a
major festival held to celebrate the beginning of
summer and its triumph over the darker powers.
Traditionally, a fire would be lit by Ireland's High
King on the summit of the Hill of Tara, and this
fire would then be used to light all other fires.

So, when St. Patrick lit a fire in advance of
High King Lóegaire's, he was deliberately inviting
the attention of the pagan chiefs. The Druid elders
were sent by Lóegaire to investigate, who reported
that Patrick's fire had magical powers because they
could not put it out. They warned that it would
burn forever if the king could not extinguish it.

King Lóegaire was unable to extinguish the
saint's fire and accepted that Patrick's "magic" was
stronger than his own. (Muirchu's *Life of Patrick*,
written two centuries later, describes a contest of
magic in which Lóegaire's Druids were forced to
concede victory to the saint.) Although he did not
choose to convert to Christianity himself, Lóegaire
was so impressed by the saint that he gave him
permission to make converts throughout his realm.
Patrick continued to travel widely in Ireland,
establishing new churches as he went, before
eventually making his headquarters in Armagh.

RIGHT: The Celtic festival of Beltane is still observed today.

THE CELTIC CROSS

This popular legend of St. Patrick is set on a day when the missionary had been preaching close to a pagan standing stone, considered sacred by his audience of potential converts because it was already carved with a circle – a mark familiar to all pagans as a symbol of the all-powerful sun.

St. Patrick is credited with inscribing a Christian (or Latin) cross through the circle, thus blessing the stone. In this way, it is said, he created the first Irish Celtic cross and showed himself willing to adapt heathen practices and symbols to Christian beliefs in order to ease the peoples' transition from paganism to Christianity. Other interpretations claim that placing the cross on top of the circle confirmed Christ's supremacy over the pagan sun.

Examples of such crosses include the Cross of Kells, Ardboe High Cross, the crosses at Monasterboice, and the Cross of the Scriptures, Clonmacnoise, as well as those in Scotland at Iona and the Kildalton Cross, which may be the earliest to survive in good condition. No examples survive from St. Patrick's time.

ABOVE & OPPOSITE: Celtic crosses are found throughout Ireland and the British Isles.

BLACKBIRDS ON CROAGH PATRICK

Rising to 2,510ft (765m) near to the town of Westport in County Mayo, the quartzite peak of Croagh Patrick was a sacred place long before the arrival of Christianity in Ireland. Croagh Patrick or Patrick's Stack, named after St. Patrick, is known locally as the "reek," a Hiberno-English word for "rick" or "stack."

For the Celtic peoples of Ireland the mountain was the dwelling place of the deity Crom Dubh and it was also the principal site of the harvest festival of Lughnasadh, a traditional Gaelic holiday celebrated on August 1, and which corresponds to the Welsh Calan Awst and the English Lammas. Lughnasadh was sacred to the god Lugh, when a funeral feast and sporting competition were held in memory of Lugh's foster-mother, Tailtiu, who died of exhaustion after singlehandedly clearing the plains of Ireland for agriculture.

According to popular Christian belief, St. Patrick spent the 40 days and 40 nights of Lent (the Christian period of fasting or self-denial, stretching from Ash Wednesday to Easter Eve) on the mountain, during which time he was harassed by demons disguised as blackbirds, the birds forming such dense clusters around him that the sky turned black. But according to this legend, he continued to pray and, at the end of his fast, Patrick threw a silver bell down the side of the mountain, knocking the she-demon Corra out of the sky. On Reek Sunday, the last Sunday in July every year, over 15,000 pilgrims climb Croagh Patrick in honor of St. Patrick, one of the 12 Apostles of Ireland.

BELOW: St. Patrick was surrounded by demons disguised as blackbirds.

OPPOSITE: Croagh Patrick, County Mayo.

IRISH SAINTS

BANISHING THE SNAKES

Probably as famous as the story of the shamrock is the legend that tells how St. Patrick drove all the snakes in Ireland into the sea where they drowned.

In many images of the saint, Patrick is seen standing on snakes, i.e., in the act of conquering them, the message being that there are no snakes in Ireland (save those in zoos) and that Patrick alone is responsible for this happy state of affairs.

It is, however, most unlikely that there ever were any snakes in Ireland! In fact, this particular legend of St. Patrick may be an allegory of the fact that snakes were sacred to the Druids, and that their banishment reflects St. Patrick's success in removing their pagan influences from the island.

THE WELL OF THE BOOK

It was St. Patrick's mission to convert the pagan Irish to Christianity, even though he was well aware of their deep hostility toward him. Knowing that his life was in great danger, Patrick knelt down before his would-be converts and prayed to God to help him save their souls. The fervor of his prayer was so great that, as the saint rose up, the mark of his knees was left deep in the stone; when the people saw the miracle they believed and listened to his words.

After this miracle, Patrick went on to the next village where the people, who believed in magic, begged for another such wonder to be performed. St. Patrick drew a great circle on the ground and bade them stand outside it; then he prayed, when the water rushed up from the earth and a well pure and bright as crystal filled the circle. As a result of this miracle, the people believed and were baptized.

The well can be seen to this day, and is called The Well of the Book (*Tober-na-Lauer*), because St. Patrick had placed his own prayer-book in the center of the circle before the water rose.

RIGHT: Located near Clonmel in Tipperary, this is another well dedicated to St. Patrick; it is fed by spring water that continually wells up from deep below the ground.

ST. CIARÁN

Born in AD 516, in County Roscommon, Connacht, Ciarán was surnamed Mac an Tsair, or "Son of the Carpenter." He was a student of St. Finian at Clonard and in time became a teacher himself. Various legends are connected with St. Ciarán, one of the most famous telling of how it was his cow – which he took with him as payment when he went to Clonard and which provided the milk for the entire monastery – which supplied the parchment for the "Book of the Dun Cow" (*Leobr na h'Uidre*), one of the oldest and most important Irish literary collections, compiled by a Clonmacnoise scribe in 1106.

In about 534, Ciarán left Clonard for Aran, where he was ordained a priest and studied under

St. Enda of Aran. Here, he received a mystical vision of a tree, laden with fruit and inhabited by birds, standing in the middle of Ireland with its branches spread out to the four corners of the land.

Enda knew Ciarán was someone special, someone who would do great things. Therefore he recognized Ciarán's vision as one of special significance, and interpreted it as a sign of Ciarán's great potential. Ciarán could be the tree, he could shelter Ireland with his grace, and feed men's spiritual hunger with his prayers and fastings. These were gifts that belonged in a wider setting, and Enda urged Ciarán to found a church on the banks of the Shannon, in the middle Ireland.

Later, in about 541, Ciarán traveled to Senan, on Scattery Island, but in 545 finally settled in Clonmacnoise, where he founded the famous monastery with ten companions. As abbot, he worked on the first buildings of the monastery but died a year later of the yellow plague, while still in his early 30s. His feast day is September 9.

BELOW & OVERLEAF: The ancient monastic site of Clonmacnoise is situated at the crossroads of Ireland on the River Shannon in County Offaly and dates back almost 1,500 years. St. Ciaran, the son of an Ulsterman who had settled in Connacht, chose the site in AD 545 because of its ideal position at the center of river and road travel in Celtic Ireland. It is surrounded by the three provinces of Connacht, Munster and Leinster.

ST. MARTIN

St. Martin's Day, November 11, also known as Martinstag or Martinmas, the Feast of St. Martin of Tours or Martin le Miséricordieux, is a time for feasting and celebrations. This is the time when autumn wheat seeding was completed, and the annual slaughter of fattened cattle produced "Martinmas beef." Historically, hiring fairs were also held where farm laborers would seek out new employment for the following year.

St. Martin started out as a Roman soldier but was baptized as an adult and became a monk. It is understood that he was a kind man who led a quiet and simple life. The most famous legend connected with him is that he once cut his cloak in half to share with a beggar during a snowstorm. That night Martin dreamt that Jesus was wearing the half-cloak he had given away, and he heard Jesus say to the angels: "Here is Martin, the Roman soldier who is not baptized; he has clothed me."

So, how did St. Martin, who was a saint widely recognized as such throughout Europe and beyond, come to be particularly revered by the Irish? Perhaps it was that St. Martin was reputed to be the uncle of St. Patrick and that it was he who gave Ireland's patron saint his monastic habit and tonsure.

A legend from County Wexford tells that fishing boats were out on the morning of St. Martin's feast day, when an apparition of the saint was seen walking on the waves. St. Martin ordered the fishermen to put their oars into the water and return to the harbor, but all those who ignored his warning perished in a storm that blew up that afternoon. Since then, no Wexford boat will put out to sea on St. Martin's Day.

It was also the custom in Wexford on November 11, that if a sheep or goat grew sick, and seemed likely to die, the farmer would put a slit in one of its ears and devote the animal to the saint. If it recovered, it would be killed and eaten on a future St. Martin's Day. It would not be sold in the interim, however, not even for ten times its value.

LEFT: A late 14th-century reliquary of St. Martin from the church at Soudeilles, Corrèze, France.

OPPOSITE: El Greco's Saint Martin and the Beggar, *ca.1600, oil on canvas. National Gallery of Art, Washington.*

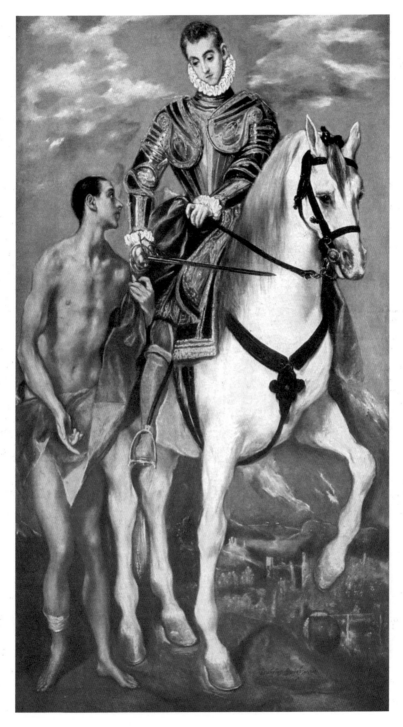

SAINT BRIGID

Although Brigid or Bride is probably the best known Irish saint after Patrick, her life cannot be documented with much certainty. Cogitosus' *Life of Brigid* was written not much more than a century after her death, but the author was mainly concerned with recounting her many miracles.

She may have been born in County Kildare, ca. AD 457, but local tradition says it was Faughart, in County Louth. Brigid's parents, Dubtach and Brocseach, may both have belonged to noble families, though it has been suggested that Brigid's mother had been a slave in Dubtach's household, though it is generally accepted that Brocseach was a Christian. Dubtach may also have been a Christian, or perhaps converted from paganism in later life.

Brigid's father may well have welcomed her decision to take the veil, once she had rejected his choice of a husband for her. With seven other young women robed in white, she took her vows before St. Mel, the abbot and bishop of Longford, and it is said that he mistakenly consecrated her a bishop.

Brigid was generous to the poor, and as a child once gave away her mother's entire store of butter. Fortunately, her prayers were answered and the butter was miraculously restored.

When seeking land for her community, she asked the king of Leinster only for as much as her cloak could cover, but the cloak miraculously spread over the entire Curragh, an area of grassland famous then as now for horse racing.

In Ireland, Christianity did not supplant paganism so much as superimpose itself on Celtic tradition, with sites of pagan worship or superstition quickly becoming associated with

OPPOSITE: St. Brigid depicted in stained glass.

BELOW: When she died, Brigid was interred to the right of the high altar of Kildare Cathedral, and a costly tomb was erected over her "adorned with gems and precious stones and crowns of gold and silver." Over the years her shrine became an object of veneration for pilgrims, especially on her feast day, February 1.

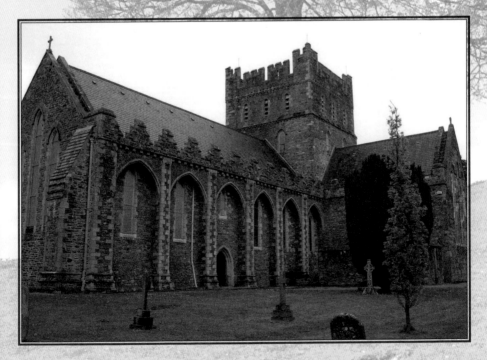

Christian worship and belief. Brigid's feast day, for example, falls on the date of Imbolc, the pagan festival of spring. Significantly, Brigid was also the name of a pagan goddess, and it even seems to have been used as a general name for Irish goddesses, for the name means "exalted one."

The attributes of the pagan Brigid, such as healing powers, learning and poetic skill, were readily perceived in the saint who established a convent at Kildare. The name Kildare means "church of the oak," and there was probably a pagan sanctuary with a sacred fire which was kept burning for centuries into the Christian era. By the time of Brigid's death in ca. 525, Kildare had become an important center of learning.

The saint traveled by chariot throughout Ireland, continuing Patrick's work of conversion, but there is no evidence that they ever met. Many miracles of healing are attributed to Brigid, such as curing lepers and restoring speech to the dumb. There are tales of her turning water into ale or stone into salt, and many speak of her rapport with animals. She also negotiated the release of captives.

Perhaps the best-known story is of her visit to a dying pagan chieftain. While she prayed, she plaited rushes into a cross. The chieftain heard her account of the cross as a Christian symbol, and was converted and baptized before he died. It is still customary on February 1 to plait St. Brigid's Crosses, in the hope that they will protect a household in the year ahead.

Brigid has been called "Mary of the Gaels" and a common salutation in the Irish language expresses the hope that "Brigid and Mary be with you." Her influence is not confined to Ireland, however, for she has been revered throughout the ages in innumerable countries. One legend tells that the medieval Knights of Chivalry chose St. Brigid as their patroness, and that it was they who first chose to call their wives "brides."

Brigid also performed miracles that seemed like curses. When on the bank of the Inny, Brigid was given a gift of apples and sweet sloes. She later entered a house where many lepers begged her for this fruit, which she willingly proferred. The nun who had given the gift to Brigid was irritated by this, in that her gift to the saint had been given away. This, in turn, angered Brigid, leading her to curse the nun's trees so that they would no longer bear fruit.

Another nun also gave Brigid the same gift, and again Brigid gave the fruit to begging lepers. This time, however, the nun asked that her garden be blessed, to which Brigid replied that a large tree in the nun's garden should thereafter bear twofold fruit, and this was done.

LEFT: These crosses are associated with Brigid of Kildare, who is venerated as one of the patron saints of Ireland. The crosses are traditionally made on February 1, which in the Irish language is called Lá Fhéile Bhríde (St. Brigid's feast day), the day on which she is celebrated in the liturgy.

Many rituals are associated with the making of the crosses, and it is believed that a Brigid's Cross protected the household from fire and evil, which is why it is seen hanging in many Irish houses.

OPPOSITE: Kildare Cathedral.

ST. COLUMBA (COLUMCILLE)

There are several accounts of Columba's life, all attesting to the miraculous signs which preceded his birth at Gartan, County Donegal, in AD 521. An angel assured his mother that she would bear a son of great beauty who would be remembered among the Lord's prophets. St. Buite, the dying abbot of Monasterboice in County Louth, is said to have foretold the birth of "a child illustrious before God and men."

Columba was of royal blood. His father Phelim was of the Uí Néill clan that included the famous Niall of the Nine Hostages, while his mother, Eithne, was descended from a king of Leinster.

It was the custom for the children of ruling families to be fostered but, unusually, Columba was given into the care of a priest. The boy's daily practice of reading the psalms led his young contemporaries to call him Columcille (Colum of

ABOVE: The west wall of St. Columba's Church at Gartan, County Donegal; Gartan is said to be the birthplace of St. Columba.

RIGHT: The beautiful Lough Gartan, near to the place of St. Columba's birth.

most famous of the latter's "12 Apostles of Ireland." Columba also spent time with a Leinster bard, named Gemman, in whose company he witnessed the murder of a young girl and vowed that, as the girl's soul went to Heaven, so the murderer's soul would go to Hell. When the murderer promptly died, Columba's reputation spread rapidly.

Columba established his first monastery at Derry in 548. Others followed, notably Durrow in County Offaly, which became famous for the Celtic artistry of its illuminated manuscripts. In 563 Columba sailed with 12 followers to found a monastery on the Scottish island of Iona, which was part of the Scottish kingdom of Dalriada, ruled by Columba's cousin Conaill.

Legend has it that Columba's exile was an act of penance, and that he deliberately chose an island out of sight of his beloved Ireland. During a visit to Moville, Columba is said to have copied a book of psalms secretly, of which Finian insisted he was given a copy. Columba refused to hand it over, and their dispute was referred to the high king, Diarmuid, who ruled: "To every cow her calf, and to every book its copy." Columba already resented Diarmuid for slaying a youth to whom the saint had given sanctuary and he persuaded his kinsmen to wage war. Diarmuid was defeated at Cuildreimhne, County Sligo, and Columba was blamed for the hundreds of dead. When a synod called on him to make amends by converting an equal number of pagans, he opted to work among the Picts of Scotland.

The extent of Columba's missionary work has probably been exaggerated by his early biographers, but there is no doubting the profound influence of Iona on the Celtic Church as a whole, and on the

the Church) and he is more usually known by that name in Ireland. He went on to study under St. Finian of Moville, County Down, where his prayers are said to have turned spring water into communion wine. He later became a pupil of St. Finian of Clonard and was destined to become the

LEFT: A depiction of St. Columba in a stained glass window in Edinburgh Castle's St. Margaret's Chapel.

OPPOSITE: Iona Abbey, on the Isle of Iona in the Inner Hebrides off the west coast of Scotland. It was founded by St. Columba in AD 563, and is considered to be one of the most important historical sites in Scotland.

spread of Christianity in Scotland and northern England. Columba was also a political figure of consequence, his early conversion of Brude, king of the Picts, having reduced the threat of attacks on Christian Dalriada. In 575, returning to Ulster for a convention at Drum Ceatt, he negotiated the Scottish kingdom's independence from the Irish Dalriada, and at the same convention persuaded King Aedh to preserve the bards of Ireland, whose satires had made them unpopular.

Columba died on Iona in 597. Chronicles of his life appeared in the following century, most notably from St. Adomnán, who attributed to him many prophecies, visions and miracles, not the least of which was the act of warding off the Loch Ness monster with the sign of the cross.

ST. KEVIN OF GLENDALOUGH

As with St. Columba, Kevin's family had noble antecedents (he was the son of Coemlog and Coemell of Leinster). According to tradition, it is said that when he was born, at the Fort of the White Fountain in AD 498, his mother felt no labor pains, and the snow that fell on the day of his birth melted as it fell around the house. An angel is said to have appeared during the child's baptism, announcing that he would be named "Kevin." St. Cronan, the officiating priest at the time, is said to have remarked, "This was surely an angel of the Lord, and as he named the child so shall he be

ABOVE: St. Kevin and the Blackbird, *a miniature of an Irish codex dated ca. 9th century* AD.

LEFT & BELOW: *St. Kevin's Bed appears to have been hollowed out by the hand of man, and is so small that only one person can conveniently stretch himself out in it. It was reputedly a retreat for St. Kevin and later for St. Laurence O'Toole.*

OPPOSITE: *The Wicklow river runs through Glendalough.*

called." So the baby was baptized Kevin – Coemgen in the Irish tongue, *pulcher-genitus* or the fair-begotten in the Latin. He was the first person in history to be called Kevin, and it is also said that he was the fulfillment of the prophecy of St. Patrick that he was the one to come who would evangelize the region of Ireland to the south of Dublin.

From the age of seven, Kevin was educated in Cornwall, living with the monks until he was 12. His earliest tutor was St. Petroc of Cornwall, who

IRELAND: LEGENDS & FOLKLORE

OPPOSITE & OVERLEAF: Glendalough, with Kevin's Kitchen (or church) in the foregound and the round tower behind.

BELOW: The upper reaches of Glendalough.

had come to Leinster in about 492, and who had devoted himself to the study of the Holy Scriptures, in which his pupil would also become proficient. Called to the monastic life, Kevin then studied for the priesthood and was tutored by St. Eonaghan. He next studied under his uncle, St. Eugenius, later Bishop of Ardstraw, who at the time lived at Kilnamanagh in Wicklow, where he passed to his pupils all the knowledge he had acquired at the famous English monastery of Rosnat.

Kevin was ordained by Bishop Lugidus, following which he lived as a hermit in a cave at Glendalough; this was a Bronze Age tomb now known as St. Kevin's Bed, to which he was reputed to have been led by an angel. Kevin habitually went barefoot, wore animal skins, ate nettles and herbs, and spent his time in prayer.

It was a lonely life, but it is said that "the branches and leaves of the trees sometimes sang sweet songs to him, and heavenly music alleviated the severity of his life." Perhaps it was in this cave, too, that Kevin learned to play his treasured harp; when he later wrote his monastic rule, it was composed in verse, and it is possible that he even set it to be accompanied by the harp.

Kevin was blessed with good looks, and unconsciously won the affections of a beautiful maiden named Kathleen, who is said to have had "eyes of the most unholy blue." Ignoring the fact that he was bound by holy vows, the bold Kathleen followed Kevin into the woods; when Kevin felt her presence, he threw himself into a bed of nettles before gathering a handful of the burning weeds and scourging the maiden with them. He is said to have remarked, "The fire without extinguishes the fire within." It seems out of character for a person as gentle as Kevin to have acted so violently, but the scourging is nothing compared with how the poets Gerald Griffin and Thomas Moore dramatized the meeting. The two works, colorful though they are,

appear to be totally imaginative and to have little bearing on the incident. Would Kevin have been likely to "hurl the maiden from the rock into the black lake shrieking," as Griffin's poem suggests? Or would he have "hurled her from the beetling rock" into the lake, as indicated in Moore's verse? Very unlikely. Especially when one considers that Kathleen later sought Kevin's forgiveness and is said to have turned her life around, becoming a woman noted for her great piety.

As with many hermits, St. Kevin had a special affection for birds and animals, which is illustrated in the *Acta Sanctorum* (Acts of the Saints), in a story about a blackbird laying an egg in Kevin's hand when his arms were outstretched in prayer. The saint remained in this position until the baby bird hatched (*see* page 72 above).

Long before his time in the cave, strange miracles had been common occurrences in Kevin's life. As an infant, a mysterious white cow is said to have come to his parent's house every morning and evening to supply the milk for the baby. Later, when Kevin was old enough, he was given the task of tending sheep. One day some men came to him and begged him to give them some sheep. He was touched by their poverty and gave them four. When evening came, however, and Kevin's sheep were counted, the correct number were still present.

On a day in autumn, Kevin was working in the kitchen. Meals were being prepared for the harvesters, when a number of pilgrims called and asked for food. Kevin, filled with compassion, gave them the harvesters' dinner, with the result that he was rebuked by his superiors. He then told the attendants to fill all the ale jars with water and gather together all the bare meat bones. Then he prayed alone and, it is said, the water turned to ale and the bones became covered again with meat.

In another story, a boar was being chased by a group of hunters with their dogs. It ran to where Kevin sat, praying under a tree, and cowered beside him for protection, but the dogs, seeing the saint in prayer, lay down and refused to approach the boar. When the hunters decided to ignore the man and kill the boar, a flock of birds settled in the tree above the praying saint. The hunters took this as a sign and left man and beast alone.

Perhaps one of the most interesting legends is that of a pet goose belonging to King O'Toole of Glendalough. Both the king and the goose were getting on in years and as time passed the goose became weak and unable to fly. Hearing of Kevin's miraculous powers, the king asked that he make the beloved goose young again. Kevin asked for a payment of whatever land the goose should fly over, and as the goose was presently flightless, O'Toole agreed. When Kevin touched the bird, it grew young and flew over the entire valley that had been used as the site for the monastery of Glendalough.

So how did the great monastery come about? History tells us that, after seven years in the cave, a farmer named Dima came upon Kevin in his hideout. Kevin yielded to Dima's persuasion to go to the place in the valley that would come to be known as Disert Coemgen. Here, disciples soon gathered around Kevin and talked him into being their spiritual leader. For a while, as the story goes, a friendly otter brought a salmon to feed Kevin and his monks every day. Then, one day the thought entered the head of farmer Dima's son that he could make a fine pair of gloves out of the otter's pelt. The otter seems to have sensed peril and suddenly disappeared, leaving the monks to fend for themselves.

Perhaps it was the lack of available food that persuaded Kevin to move farther up the glen, at the junction of two sparkling streams, but it is here that he established his permanent monastery. He was also reported, around this time, to have made a pilgrimage to Rome to bring back the blessing of the Pope to his community.

It was at the new site of Glendalough that Kevin and his monks began to erect the first rough churches, cells and round tower that would make the settlement a center of prayer and

pilgrimage, and its very ruins a memorable sight even to this day.

In his time, the charismatic and kindly St. Kevin attracted many visitors to Glendalough. One tale tells how King Colman of the Faelain, having lost his earlier sons by deaths that he blamed on evil spirits, entrusted his next infant son, Faelan, to the care of the saintly abbot. Now the monastery had no cows to provide milk for the child, but Kevin, on encountering a doe, commanded her to nurse the little prince along with her fawn. When that source of nourishment ceased, St. Kevin ordered a she-wolf to assume the task with which she complied.

Other boys were also sent to the monks to be educated. On a certain day one of them asked for an apple. The monastery had no more apple trees than it had cows, but St. Kevin blessed a clump of willow trees and the willows began to bear apples; four centuries later, these miraculous trees were still producing "St. Kevin's apples."

Kevin also planted a yew tree at the door of what would be, from the 12th to the 15th centuries, the cathedral church of Glendalough. This yew was particularly revered as such until 1835, when a neighboring landowner chopped it down to make furniture. Devotees of St. Kevin hastened to collect every last chip of the wood as relics of the venerable founder.

Still another story is told regarding the actual construction of the cathedral when, it is said, the laborers and masons agreed to work as long a day as possible and to "rise with the lark and lie with the lamb." These long hours soon had the men exhausted and when Kevin investigated he found that the local larks began their day extremely early. He prayed for an answer to the problem and from that day, according to tradition, the skylark ceased to sing in Glendalough.

As word of Kevin's holiness spread, Glendalough became the "parent" of several other monastic foundations. After visiting Sts. Columba, Comgall and Cannich at Usneach in Westmeath, Kevin proceeded to Clonmacnoise, where St.

Ciáran had died three days earlier, in ca. 546. Having firmly established his community, he retired into solitude for four years, and only returned to Glendalough at the earnest entreaty of his monks. So numerous were his followers that Glendalough became a veritable city in the desert.

Kevin belonged to the second order of Irish saints and as such was probably never a bishop, but Glendalough was later an episcopal see, although it is now incorporated with Dublin. St. Kevin's house and St. Kevin's Bed of rock are still to be seen: and the Seven Churches of Glendalough have for centuries been visited by pilgrims from all over the world.

Widely noted though he was, St. Kevin was always a hermit and a pilgrim at heart, and disliked being tied down. Even in his old age he had a yearning to make just one more pilgrimage. When he mentioned his desire to a wise old man, however, he replied that "Birds do not hatch their eggs when they are on the wing." Kevin took that as a sign from God that he should stay where he was.

St. Kevin died in 618 of natural causes and was canonized in 1903. His feast day is celebrated on June 3, also sometimes known as Pattern Day in Glendalough or simply "Pattern," which is the general term for a designated date honoring the local patron saint. After the British had all but destroyed the celebrated community in 1398, the Irish and others still came and prayed in the name of St. Kevin. After the Dissolution of the Monasteries in 1539, when the community was closed down as an official church site, the ever-faithful followers of St. Kevin came every June 3 to celebrate the memory of the great teacher and holy man. In fact, the Feast of St. Kevin had become such a riotous event by the 18th and 19th centuries (the peak of the St. Kevin's Day frenzy), that the church, which frowned on such joyous revelry (at least officially), banned the festival in the 1890s.

As might be expected, St. Kevin, the "St. Francis of Ireland," is the patron saint of blackbirds.

OPPOSITE: The round tower at Glendalough.

SAINT BRENDAN

One of the 12 Apostles of Ireland, St. Brendan (Bréanainn) of Clonfert (ca. 484–ca. 577), called "the Navigator," "the Voyager," or "the Bold," is one of the early Irish monastic saints. He is renowned chiefly for his legendary quest to the "Land of Promise," also called Saint Brendan's Island. St. Brendan's feast day is celebrated on May 16.

Brendan was born in Ciarraighe Luachra, near to the port of Tralee, in County Kerry, and was baptized at Tubrid, near Ardfert. For five years he was educated under the mystical St. Ita, "the Brigid of Munster," and completed his studies under her brother, St. Erc, who ordained him a priest in 512. From then until 530 Brendan built monastic cells at Ardfert and at the foot of Mount Brandon, Shanakeel (Seana Cill), usually translated as "the old church," also called Baalynevinoorach.

While much of Brendan's missionary work is documented, the details of his other exploits can be regarded as widely speculative. Some say that Brendan's passion for sea travel had been nurtured by a childhood spent on the coast, and that it was this that led him to travel as far west as Iceland, Greenland, and perhaps to the shores of North America. These missionary travels led him to construct boats known as curraghs (or currachs), which were made by stretching animal skins over wooden frames. He would have been accompanied by as many as 60 monks on his travels throughout the British Isles and Northern France, during which he is said to have met St. Columba on Hynba Island in Scotland, traveled to Brittany with the Welsh monk, St. Malo (one of the seven founder saints of Brittany), and to have visited the Welsh monastery of Llancarfan founded by St. Cadoc.

Brendan's missionary journeys, however, often pale into insignificance when compared with his legendary seven-year journey to the Land of Promise. While meditating in a chapel at the peak of what is now Mount Brandon, Brendan is said to

RIGHT: St. Brendan built monastic cells at Ardfert and at the foot of Mount Brandon (Brendon's Mount).

have experienced a vision of Hy-Brasil, the legendary Land of Promise. He constructed a 36-ft curragh and, after fasting for 40 days, set out with a crew of more than 12 men from Dingle Bay.

According to the *Navigatio Sancti Brendani*, a Latin prose work written by the beginning of the 10th century by an Irish author, Brendan's vision of the Land of Promise was inspired by the boasts of another abbot, who lived in the north of Ireland and who claimed to have visited it many times by traveling only a short distance over the North Atlantic Ocean. Without any navigational aids, Brendan and his crew set out, trusting that God would guide their craft to their desired destination. On their travels, they encounter Judas Iscariot, who allowed a temporary reprieve from Hell,

clings to a rock above the sea. They also enjoy a conversation with the spirit of St. Patrick.

During their voyage, the travelers encounter floating crystal palaces, "mountains in the sea spouting fire," and sea monsters with cat-like heads and horns emanating from their mouths, which could be translated as icebergs, volcanoes and walruses, indicating that Brendan made it at least as

OPPOSITE: A stained-glass image of St. Brendan in the church dedicated to him at Birr, County Offaly.

ABOVE: A woodcut of a scene from Navigatio Sancti Brendani, *showing the saint celebrating Easter Mass on the body of a whale.*

LEFT: St. Brendan depicted on a medieval map close to an island bearing his name. No such island exists on modern maps but it was said to have been located close to the Canary Islands.

far as Iceland, which is supported elsewhere in the *Navigatio* when Brendan visits an island inhabited by former seekers of the Land of Promise. The island, inhabited by the Irish monks of the Community of Ailbe, is described as containing warm muddy pools and crystal, which some believe may be the natural hot springs and ice spar of Iceland.

In another part of the *Navigatio*, the story of Jasconius is related; Jasconius is a whale mistaken for an island by Brendan and his crew, who realize their mistake when they light a fire on the surprised animal's back. But Jasconius eventually befriends the monks, allowing them to conduct Easter Mass on his back for seven consecutive years. In other parts of the tale, the monks arrive in a tropical climate, visiting islands that may be fictional or, as some scholars suggest, may also be the Canary Islands, Jamaica or the Bahamas. These islands featured "grapes as big as apples," which could possibly be oranges or grapefruit. The journey concludes when the crew returns to Donegal Bay after sailing through lands and bodies of water that resemble Newfoundland, Greenland and Iceland in their respective descriptions.

The *Navigatio Sancti Brendani* was widely translated and distributed throughout Europe during the Middle Ages, leading some cartographers and explorers to take it for fact and include St. Brendan's Island on maps of the era.

Whether Brendan actually reached North America remains a mystery but, in 1976, the explorer Tim Severin built a curragh that he named after the saint and, in the same manner as Brendan, traversed the North Atlantic to the Faroe Islands (believed to be the Island of Sheep that Brendan described) and wintered in Iceland. Severin eventually landed in Newfoundland in June 1977, proving at least the possibility of Brendan's voyage to North America.

LEFT: A 15th-century wood carving in Clonfert Cathedral depicting a mermaid with a comb and mirror, which can be interpreted as a reference to an incident that St. Brendan and his crew experienced on a voyage. To quote one of the surviving texts: "When all this was over at last, they resumed their journey and once more got into great difficulties, because they saw a beast coming towards them with a human body and face, but from the waist downwards it was a fish. It is called a siren, a very lovely creature with a beautiful human shape; it sings so well and its voice is so sweet that whoever hears it cannot resist sleep and does not know what he is doing. When this sea monster approached them, the shipmen fell asleep and let the ship drift: the monks too forgot themselves completely because of its voice and did not know where they were."

OPPOSITE: Clonfert Cathedral in County Galway. The original monastery was founded here by St. Brendan in AD 563 and it is here that the great navigator is buried.

CHAPTER THREE
THE HIGH KINGS OF IRELAND

The High Kings of Ireland (*Ard Rí na hÉireann*) were sometimes legendary, sometimes historical figures who had, or are claimed to have had, dominion over the whole of Ireland. Medieval and early modern Irish literature portrays an almost unbroken sequence of High Kings ruling from Tara over a hierarchy of lesser kings that stretches back thousands of years.

The list of High Kings of Ireland goes back thousands of years, probably to the second millennium BC, and is quite vast. While some earlier parts of the list may be classed as mythical, it is unclear at what point historical individuals begin to be included, and also when these individuals can genuinely be said to be "High Kings" in the later sense of the word. The names of some individuals crop up very much more frequently than others, and have tended, consequently, to make more of an impact on the history of Ireland.

In the early narrative literature, kingship is sacral: a king is symbolically married to the sovereign goddess, Medb (Maeve); he also has to be free from blemish, he enforces symbolic *buada* (prerogatives) and avoids symbolic *geasa* (singular *geis* – idiosyncratic taboos, whether of obligation or prohibition, similar to being under a vow or spell). Inaugurations were held at places such as the Hill of Tara, the seat of the High King and a sacral site, at the Lia Fáil (Stone of Destiny), while other, lesser, kings would be inaugurated all over Ireland in such

places as Doon Rock in County Donegal. These kings ruled over their local region and often fought with other kings.

The duties and responsibilities of the High Kings were to rule the boundaries of their own kingdoms; they would have been responsible for ensuring good government by exercising *fir flaithemon* (rulers' truth). Their responsibilities would have included convening popular assemblies, collecting taxes, building public works, maintaining external relations, defense, emergency legislation, law enforcement, and promulgating legal judgements.

By the 12th century the dual process of amassing territory and consolidating kingship saw the handful of remaining provincial kings abandoning the traditional royal sites for the cities, employing ministers and governors, receiving advice from an *oireacht* (a body of noble counsellors), presiding at reforming synods and maintaining standing armies.

Early royal succession had been by alternation between collateral branches of the wider dynasty but succession was now confined to a series of father/son, brother/brother and uncle/nephew successions within a small royal line marked by an exclusive surname. These families, which included the O'Brien of Munster, MacLochlainn of the North, and O'Connor of Connacht, intermarried and competed against one another for many years. The most famous High King, and one who is remembered to this day, is Brian Boru.

OPPOSITE: The Stone of Destiny (Lia Fáil) is a sacral site on the Hill of Tara.

ABOVE: An aerial view of the Hill of Tara, the ancient seat of the High Kings of Ireland.

OVERLEAF: Meascán Méabha (Medb's Cairn, Tomb or Grave), bears the name of Medb or Maeve, the sovereign goddess to whom all kings of Ireland were symbolically married. It stands on the summit of Knocknarea, in County Sligo, and is the largest cairn in Ireland outside Brú na Bóinne.

BRIAN BORU: THE LAST KING OF IRELAND

Brian Bóruma mac Cennétig, ca. 941–April 23, 1014, ended the domination of the High Kingship of Ireland by the Uí Néill. Building on the achievements of his father, Cennétig mac Lorcain, and especially his older brother, Mathgamain, Brian first made himself king of Munster, then subjugated Leinster, becoming the ruler of the south of Ireland.

When Brian was a child, Viking invaders often attacked Ireland, and many of the Irish people

RIGHT & OPPOSITE: Two very different portrayals of Brian Boru.

BELOW: The Rock of Cashel was the traditional seat of the kings of Munster for several hundred years prior to the Norman invasion. In 1101, the king of Munster, Muircheartach Ua Briain, donated his fortress on the rock to the Catholic Church.

either sided with the Norsemen or belonged to small kingdoms that fought among themselves constantly. King Mathgamain wanted peace with the Vikings and tried to achieve it, but Brian Boru desired the opposite; he hated the Vikings because, when he was still young, he had witnessed the death of his mother and much of the Dal Cais (Delcassian) tribe in a Norse raid. Consequently, when he was old enough, Boru broke away from his brother to wage guerrilla warfare on the Norse. A skilled negotiator, he was able to win many important victories that made the Vikings greatly fear the Irish.

Boru's attacks also helped spread rumors that there was a large, secret Delcassian army. Boru's campaign gained much popular support and many Irishmen joined him, including his brother, Mathgamain, who by now no longer sought peace with the Vikings. These joined forces were able to drive most of the Norse from southern Ireland, including their leader Ivar (also known as Imar).

Ten years later, Ivar returned and captured and killed King Mathgamain, with the result that Brian Boru became king of Munster. Soon after, his army met with that of Ivar and Brian challenged Ivar to a duel. Ivar was killed and, for a short time, the Viking influence in southern Ireland was shattered. Boru's power continued to grow throughout southern Ireland and he rebuilt many of the churches and other monuments that had been destroyed by the Norsemen.

Further north, Malachy II's forces defeated a Norse army that had been trying to take Dublin in 980, after which Malachy became king of Meath. The two kings, Malachy and Brian, met in 998 and agreed to divide Ireland between them, with Boru receiving the south and Malachy the north. But Boru had too much support, even in northern Ireland, so Malachy eventually allowed Boru to take northern Ireland peacefully. Boru was granted the

The power of the Vikings in Ireland was broken for good at the Battle of Clontarf, though Brian Boru lost his own life in the process.

title High King, making him one of the first kings to unite Ireland successfully under one monarch.

But many people opposed Brian Boru, such as some native Irish and the remaining Norse. In 1013, Maelmordha, King of Leinster, revolted against Boru and allied with the Vikings, making an army from Boru's other Irish rivals and with warriors from Viking nations as far away as Normandy and Iceland.

On Good Friday 1014, the forces of the Norse and rebel Irish met with those of Brian Boru at the Battle of Clontarf, where nearly 4,000 Irishmen were killed, including Brian's son Murrough, but the Viking and Leinster forces suffered even heavier losses. Brian's troops proved unexpectedly powerful, however, and they won the day. At the end of the battle, what little remained of the Norse forces retreated to their ships. But before all the invaders could flee, a small group of Norsemen went to Brian's tent and decided that if they couldn't have Ireland they would at least kill the High King. Brian was able to kill several of the men but King Brodar of Man struck Boru a mortal wound.

Other accounts, however, tell that Brian's sons led the Irish army to the decisive victory over the Vikings, and that Brian, who was too old to fight, was awaiting news of the battle when he was slain in his tent by a Viking intruder. Yet another source tells that Brian Boru was praying in his tent after the battle when a Viking stabbed him from behind.

With the death of High King Brian Boru, Ireland soon fell into chaos and rebellion, and there would never be another king powerful enough to rule all of Ireland. But Boru ended 200 years of domination by the Norsemen. His rule was a "Golden Age" of building, restoration of the Church and the development of Irish culture.

Today, Boru is also known as the founder of the Clan O Brien as well as being the inspiration for one of the symbols most commonly associated with Ireland; the harp is also used as Guinness's beer logo.

OPPOSITE LEFT: An engraving depicting the death of Brian Boru at the hands of a Viking.

OPPOSITE RIGHT: The Trinity Harp, in Trinity College, Dublin, is also known as Brian Boru's Harp, but is not of the right period to have ever belonged to him.

ABOVE: A Viking longship.

According to Celtic myth, the Gaelic harp owned by Brian Boru was once the property of the Dagda (*see* pages 16 & 17, The Dagda's Harp). There is another harp bearing Brian's name, this being one of three surviving medieval harps dating from the 14th or 15th centuries which is displayed at Trinity College, Dublin.

CHAPTER FOUR
IRISH FAIRIES

THE SIDHE

The beings known as the Sidhe, the people of the mounds, or alternatively the Lordly Ones or the Good People, are said to be descended from the Tuatha Dé Danann (the People of Danu), who settled in Ireland millennia ago and, on their defeat by the Milesians, retreated to a dimension of space and time that differs from our own. In general,

BELOW: Fairy Castle is the peak of Two Rock in Dun Laoghaire-Rathdown. It is the remains of a passage tomb, the easternmost of a series of cairns that stretches across the Dublin and Wicklow Mountains. Cairns are also known as raths and are said to be inhabited by the Sidhe.

OPPOSITE: Midsummer Eve, ca. 1908, by Edward Robert Hughes (1851–1914).

there seem to be two types of Sidhe: the lordly, spirit-like beings that resemble beautiful human beings, and those such as leprechauns, pookas, merrows and banshees. Clearly the belief in the Sidhe is a remnant of the pre-Christian religion which survived for thousands of years and which never became completely eradicated from the minds of the people.

Today, the Sidhe are still believed to inhabit earthen mounds and fairy raths and cairns – also Tír na nÓg, a mythical island to the west of Ireland. Irish placenames prefixed Lis, Rath, Shee, etc., for example, Lismore, Lisdoonvarna, Sheemore and Rathfarnham, have traditional associations with this race. Daoine Sidhe (pronounced deenee shee) means fairy folk, and many consider the Sidhe to be the genuine article.

In the "Book of the Dun Cow" (*Leobr na h'Uidre*) and the *Book of Leinster*, the Sidhe are described as "gods and not gods," which indicates that they are "something in between."

LEFT: The Fairy Wood, *1903, by Henry Meynell Rheam (1859–1920).*

OVERLEAF: Lismore Castle. *Lismore, meaning "great ring fort" is a town in County Waterford on the River Blackwater, the prefix "Lis" indicating that it has associations with the fairy folk.*

THE BANSHEE

The *bean-sidhe* (woman of the fairy) has been described as an ancestral spirit whose role is to forewarn members of certain ancient Irish families of an impending death. According to tradition, the banshee follows five families: the O'Neills, the O'Briens, the O'Connors, the O'Gradys and the Kavanaghs, although intermarriage has since augmented this select list.

Whatever her origins, the banshee may appear in one of three guises: as a young woman, a stately matron or as a raddled old hag, i.e., as Badhbh, Macha or the Morrigan (Mor-Rioghain), which are the triple aspects of the Celtic goddess of war and death. Usually, the banshee wears either a gray, hooded cloak or the winding sheet or shroud of the unshriven dead. She may also appear as a washerwoman, and can be seen apparently washing the blood-stained clothing of those who are about to die. In this guise she is known as the *bean-nighe* (washerwoman).

Although not always seen, her mourning call can clearly be heard, usually at night, when someone is about to die. In 1437, King James I of Scotland was approached by an Irish seeress, an example of the banshee in human form, who foretold his murder at the instigation of the Earl of Atholl. There are records of several human

banshees or prophetesses attending the great houses of Ireland and the courts of local Irish kings. In some parts of Leinster she is referred to as the *bean chaointe* (keening woman), whose wail is so piercing that it can shatter glass. In Kerry, the keening is experienced as "low, pleasant singing;" in Tyrone as "the sound of two boards being struck together;" and on Rathlin Island as "a thin, screeching sound somewhere between the wail of a woman and the moan of an owl."

The banshee may also appear in a variety of other forms, such as those of a hooded crow, stoat, hare or weasel – all animals that are associated with witchcraft in Ireland.

ABOVE: The Banshee (La Belle Dame sans Merci), 1901, by Henry Meynell Rheam (1859–1920).

LEFT: The banshee sometimes appears clad in a gray hooded cloak.

OPPOSITE: This 17th-century gargoyle on a tomb possibly depicts a screaming woman or a banshee.

LEFT: In legend, the keening of the banshee is heard when someone is about to die. There are particular families that are believed to have banshees following them, and whose cries herald the death of a member of that family. In Kerry, in the southwest of Ireland, the banshee's warning cry is unusually experienced as "low, pleasant singing."

THE CHANGELING

It appears that fairy women find giving birth a difficult and painful experience. Many fairy children die before birth and those that do survive are sometimes stunted or deformed. Satisfied only with offspring that are aesthetically pleasing, fairies are repelled by these infants and have no wish to keep them. Consequently, they will attempt to swap them for healthy human children, who are stolen from the mortal world.

The wizened, ill-tempered creature left in place of the human child is generally known as a changeling and possesses the power to introduce evil into a household. Any child who is unbaptized, or who is excessively admired, is at particular risk of being exchanged.

Changelings, however, are betrayed by their temperament. Human babies are generally joyful and pleasant creatures, but the fairy substitute is never happy, except when some calamity is befalling the household. For the most part, it howls and screeches throughout its waking hours and the sound and frequency of its howls often challenge the bounds of mortal endurance.

A changeling can be one of three types: an actual fairy child; a senile fairy disguised as a child; or inanimate objects, such as pieces of wood which take on the appearance of a child through fairy magic. This latter type is known as a stock.

IRELAND: LEGENDS & FOLKLORE

Puckered and wizened features, coupled with yellow, parchment-like skin, are all changeling attributes. This fairy will also have very deep, dark eyes which betray a wisdom far beyond its apparent years, and may display other characteristics, usually physical deformities, among which a crooked back or twisted hand are common. About two weeks after their arrival in the human household, changelings will also exhibit a full set of teeth, legs

as thin as chicken bones, and hands which are curved and crooked as birds' talons and covered with a light, downy hair.

No luck can come to a family in which there is a changeling; this is because the creature drains away all the good fortune that would normally attend the household. Thus, families that are so-cursed will tend to become poor as a result of their desperate struggle to maintain the ravenous monster in their midst.

One positive feature which this fairy may demonstrate, however, is an aptitude for music. As it begins to grow, the changeling may take up an instrument, often the fiddle or the Irish pipes, and will play with such skill that all who hear it will be entranced. This report is from near Boho in County Fermanagh:

I saw a changeling one time. He lived with two oul' brothers away beyond the Dog's Well and looked like a wee

wizened monkey. He was about ten or eleven but he couldn't really walk, just bobbed about. But he could play the whistle the best that you ever heard. Old tunes that the people has long forgotten, that was all he played. Then one day, he was gone and I don't know what happened to him at all.

Prevention being better than cure, a number of protections may be placed around a human infant's cradle to ward off the possibility of an exchange. A holy crucifix or iron tongs placed across the cradle will usually prove effective,

because fairies have an innate fear of these objects, while an article of the father's clothing, laid across the child as it sleeps, will have the same effect.

Changelings have prodigious appetites and will eat all that is set before them. The changeling has teeth and claws and does not take the breast like a human infant, but steals food from the larder and, when it has finished each meal, will demand more. Changelings have been known to eat the cupboard bare and still not be satisfied, yet no matter how much they devour, will remain as scrawny as ever.

found is a blackened twig or a piece of bog oak where the body of the infant should have been. Some live longer but rarely into their teens.

There can also be adult changelings. These fairy doubles will exactly replicate the person taken but will have sour dispositions. The double will be cold and aloof and take no interest in friends or family. It will also be argumentative and scolding. As with an infant, a marked personality change is a strong indication of an adult changeling.

Changelings may be driven from a house and, if this can be achieved, then the human child or adult will invariably be returned unharmed. The least severe method of expulsion is to trick the fairy into revealing its true age. Another method is to force tea made from lusmore (foxglove) down its throat, burning out its human entrails and forcing it to flee back to the fairy realm. Heat and fire are anathema to the changeling and will promptly cause it to fly away.

Changelings do not live long in the mortal world, but usually shrivel up and die within two or three years. The changeling is mourned and buried, but if its grave is ever disturbed all that will be

ABOVE: The Fairy Raid: Carrying off a Changeling – Midsummer Eve, *by Sir Joseph Noel Paton (1821–1901).*

RIGHT: Forcing a changeling to drink a tea infused with foxglove will encourage it to return whence it came.

DOBHAR-CHÚ

The dobhar-chú is an old Irish cryptid, or being whose existence is disputed or unsubstantiated, that is said to resemble either an otter, a dog/fish hybrid, or a serpentine creature, though in all forms it is commonly described as having fur with protective properties like that of an otter. It can range from white to brown or black in color.

The dobhar-chú is said to reside in lakes but has the capability of walking quite fast on land (in one tale it is said to be able to keep up with horses). It is known to attack human beings for food.

There are at least two well-known grave sites associated with the dobhar-chú. The first is the Kinlough stone, said to mark the burial place of a woman killed by the dobhar-chú, and which even provides an image of the creature. The second is the Glenade stone by Lake Glenade, where a woman was reputed to have been killed in similar circumstances in 1722, and where there is also a drawing of the beast.

Taken from a book by Patrick Tohall, the story goes as follows:

A woman named Gráinne [Grace], wife of a man called McLoghlin, who lived with her husband in the townland of Creevelea at the northwest corner of Glenade Lake, took some clothes down to the lakeshore to wash them. When she did not return, her husband went to look for her and found her bloody body by the lakeside with the *dobhar-chú asleep on her breast. Returning to the house for his dagger, he stole silently up on the dobhar-chú and drove the knife into its breast. Before it died, however, it*

TOP: *An artist's impression of a dobhar-chú, shown as half-dog, half-serpent.*

LEFT: *This old engraving portrays the dobhar-chú in yet another guise.*

ABOVE: *The Glenade stone marks the grave of Gráinne or Grace, who was killed by the dobhar-chú.*

OPPOSITE: *The otter is most commonly described as resembling the dobhar-chú, the word dobharchú also being Irish for otter.*

whistled to call its fellow; and the old people of the place, who knew the ways of the animals, warned McLoghlin to fly for his life. He took to horse, another mounted man accompanying him. The second dobhar-chú came out from the lake and pursued the pair who, realizing that they could not shake it off, stopped near some old walls and drew their horses across a door opening. The dobhar-chú rushed under the horses' legs to attack the men, but as it emerged from beneath them one of the men stabbed and killed it.

Though in some versions of the tale the latter beast had a horn with which it ran the horses through, it should be noted that the modern Irish word for "otter" is indeed *dobharchú*.

THE DULLAHAN

The dullahan, also durahan or *gan ceann* (without a head), is a type of unseelie (malevolent) fairy. It is usually seen carrying its head under one arm, and rides a headless black horse. The head's eyes are massive and constantly dart about like flies, while the mouth is fixed in a hideous grin that stretches from ear to ear. The flesh of the head is said to have the color and appearance of moldy cheese.

The dullahan's whip is actually the spine of a human corpse, and the wagon or hearse it sometimes uses is furnished with macabre objects, such as candles in skulls, wheel spokes made from thighbones, and a pall that has been chewn by worms. The dullahan stops riding at the place where a person is due to die, calling out their name, at which point the person will promptly perish.

There is no way of shutting out a dullahan for, as it approaches, all locks and gates open of their own accord. They do not appreciate being watched while on their errands, but throw basinfuls of blood on those who dare to do so (often a mark that they're among the next to die), or even lashing out the watchers' eyes with their whips. They are afraid of gold, however, and even a single golden pin can drive a dullahan away. The myth of the dullahan may have inspired the "Headless Horseman" in the *Legend of Sleepy Hollow*.

Another legendary parallel is the Green Knight, in the medieval story "Sir Gawain and the Green Knight," who is otherworldly, greenish in color, hostile, determined to take Sir Gawain's life and, after Sir Gawain strikes him, headless. This story has antecedents in the ancient "Feast of Bricriu," with the legendary Irish warrior Cú Chulainn in the role later played by Sir Gawain.

The dullahan is portrayed in fantasy fiction and video games as a beheaded knight, who carries his severed head under one arm while viciously attacking interlopers to the place that it haunts. It also has the ability to breathe fire from its severed head, or alternately may be an animated suit of armor.

OPPOSITE ABOVE: The story of Sir Gawain and the Green Knight may have been inspired by tales of the dullahan or headless horseman.

OPPOSITE BELOW: The dullahan is depicted here as a headless horse and rider.

ABOVE: The 18th-century Philipsburg Manor, in Sleepy Hollow, New York. The Legend of Sleepy Hollow, despite having a basis in German folklore, also contains echoes of the story of the dullahan.

THE GRANT

The grant is a small fairy horse that features in the
folklore of both Ireland and Britain. It warns of
approaching danger, uttering piercing cries to warn
others of its kind or mortals who may have tamed it.
Grants are most often found in dense forests and are
extremely shy.

In England, a grant may adopt a particular
village and has been described as resembling a
yearling foal with sparkling eyes. He prances about
the village streeets at midday or sunset, often
capering along on his hind legs and setting the dogs
barking. Those who see him fear that their houses will
catch fire or that a imilar misfortune may occur.

In 1211 Gervase of Tilbury described the grant
as a demon, having already pronounced it to be a
harbinger of death. But during the Second World
War, several villages claimed to have been warned of
approaching air raids by their fairy horses.

RIGHT: The grant is a young, prancing fairy horse.

THE GROGOCH

Grogochs were half-human, half-fairy beings who came from Kintyre in Scotland to settle in Ireland. Grogochs, well-known throughout northern Antrim, Rathlin Island and parts of Donegal, may also be found on the Isle of Man, where they are known as *phynnodderee*. Resembling very small, elderly men, though covered in coarse, dense reddish hair or fur, they wear no clothes but various twigs and dirt cling to their bodies as a result of their bucolic lifestyle. Grogochs are not noted for their personal hygiene and females of the species are never to be seen.

The grogoch is impervious to searing heat or freezing cold, and his home may be a cave, hollow or a simple cleft in a rock. In many parts of the northern countryside, large leaning stones are reputed to be grogochs' houses.

The grogoch has the power to make himself invisible and will only allow certain trusted people to observe him. Being a sociable being, he may even attach himself to certain human individuals and help them with their planting and harvesting or with domestic chores, for which no payment is demanded other than a jug of cream.

He likes to scuttle about the kitchen, looking for odd jobs to do, and will invariably get under people's feet in the process. Like many other fairies,

the grogoch has a great fear of the clergy and will not enter a house if a priest or minister is there. Therefore, if a grogoch is starting to make a nuisance of himself, invite a clergyman into the house who will drive the creature away, encouraging him to go torment someone else instead.

OPPOSITE: The grogoch means well but can become a nuisance when it attaches itself to a person's home.

THE LEPRECHAUN

The word "leprechaun" may have derived from the Irish *leath bhrogan* (shoemaker), although its origins may lie in *luacharma'n* (Irish for pygmy). These apparently aged little men, are frequently to be found in an intoxicated state, the result of drinking home-brewed poteen. But they never get so drunk that their hand on the hammer becomes unsteady and their work impaired.

Leprechauns seem to have made themselves the self-appointed guardians of ancient treasure (left by the Danes in their maraudings through Ireland), burying it in crocks or pots. This may be why leprechauns tend to avoid contact with humans, whom they regard as foolish, flighty and greedy creatures. If caught by a mortal, the leprechaun will promise great wealth if allowed to go free. He carries two leather pouches, in one of

OPPOSITE ABOVE: Leprechauns use gold as bribery.

OPPOSITE BELOW & RIGHT: A leprechaun is a type of fairy who usually appears as a diminutive old man, clad in a red or green coat, who likes making shoes as well as mischief. Like other fairy creatures, leprechauns have been closely linked with the Tuatha Dé Danann of Irish mythology.

which there is a silver shilling, a magical coin that returns to the purse each time it is paid out. In the other is a gold coin which the leprechaun uses to bribe his way out of difficult situations, and which usually turns to leaves or ashes once the leprechaun has parted with it. One must never, ever take one's eyes off a leprechaun, for he can is sure to vanish in the twinkling of an eye.

The leprechaun "family" appears to split into two distinct groups: leprechaun and cluricaun. Cluricauns may steal or borrow almost anything, creating mayhem in houses during the hours of darkness, raiding wine cellars and larders. They will also harness sheep, goats, dogs and even domestic fowl and ride them throughout the countryside at night. Although the leprechaun has been described as Ireland's national fairy, the name was originally used only in the north Leinster area. Variants of the name include *lurachmain*, *lurican* or *lurgadhan*.

THE MERROW

Merrows are specifically female entities, and the word "merrow" or *moruadh* comes from the Irish *muir* (meaning sea) and *oigh* (meaning maid). Mermen – the merrows' male counterparts – are rarely to be seen, but have been described as exceptionally ugly and scaly, with pig-like features and long, pointed teeth. Merrows themselves are extraordinarily beautiful and are promiscuous in their relationships with mortals.

The Irish merrow differs physically from a human being in that her feet are flatter and her hands are slightly webbed between the fingers. It should never be assumed that merrows are kindly and well-disposed toward human beings for, as members of the Sidhe, or fairy world, the inhabitants of Tir fo Thoinn (the Land Beneath the Waves) have a natural antipathy toward mankind. In some parts of Ireland they are even regarded as bringers of misfortune and harbingers of death.

The merrow has special clothing that enables her to travel through ocean currents. In Kerry, Cork and Wexford, she wears a small red cap of

BELOW: The merrow is exceptionally beautiful and can be tricked into forming relationships with mortal men, even though her true home will always be the sea.

OPPOSITE: Merrows are often wealthy, having hidden away caches of gold plundered from shipwrecks.

feathers, called a *cohullen druith*. In more northerly waters, however, she traverses the seas wrapped in a sealskin cloak, and could easily be mistaken for a seal. In order to come ashore, the merrow must abandon her cap or cloak but cannot return to the sea without them. Therefore, any mortal finding these objects will have power over the merrow, and may even persuade her to marry them by hiding the objects where they can never be found. Such fairy brides are often extremely wealthy, in that they may have caches of gold, plundered from shipwrecks, hidden away. Sometimes the merrow is able to recover her cap or cloak, when her urge to return to the sea will prove so strong that she will abandon her human husband and children forever.

IRELAND: LEGENDS & FOLKLORE

Many coastal dwellers have taken merrows as lovers, and a number of famous Irish families claim their descent from such unions, notably the O'Flaherty and O'Sullivan families of Kerry and the MacNamaras of Clare. The Irish poet, W. B. Yeats, reported a further case in his *Irish Fairy and Folk Tales*: "Near Bantry in the last century, there is said to have been a woman, covered in scales like a fish, who was descended from such a marriage." Despite their wealth and beauty, one should be particularly wary when it comes getting oneself entangled with such creatures.

THE POOKA

No fairy is more feared in Ireland than the pooka, possibly because it is always out and about at night, seeking to do harm and make mischief, and because it can assume a variety of terrifying forms.

The guise in which it most often appears is that of a sleek, dark horse with sulfur-yellow eyes and a long wild mane. In this form, it roams large areas of the countryside at night, tearing down fences and gates, scattering livestock, trampling crops and generally causing mayhem in the vicinity of remote farms.

In lonely areas of County Down, the pooka becomes a small, deformed goblin who demands a share of the crop at the end of the harvest: for this reason, what is known as the "pooka's share" is left behind for it by the reapers. In parts of County Laois, the pooka becomes a huge, hairy bogeyman, terrifying anyone who is abroad at night; in Waterford and Wexford it appears as an eagle with a massive wingspan; and in Roscommon as a black goat with curly horns.

The mere sight of a pooka may prevent hens from laying or cows from giving milk, and it is the curse of all late-night travelers as it is known to scoop them up onto its back before throwing them into muddy ditches or bogholes. The pooka has the power of human speech, and has been known to stop in front of certain houses and call out the names of those it wants to take upon its midnight forays. If they refuse, then the pooka will proceed to vandalize their property in an orgy of vindictive fury.

The origins of the pooka are to some extent speculative. The name may come from the Scandinavian *pook* or *puke*, meaning "nature spirit." Such beings are most capricious and have to be continually placated. Alternatively, it may have been the horse cults, prevalent throughout the early Celtic world, that gave rise to the pooka as a nightmare steed, though other authorities suggest the name comes from the early Irish *poc*, meaning either "a male goat" or a "blow from a cudgel." The

horse theory is perhaps the most plausible, however, since members of many of these horse cults met on high ground and the main abode of the pooka is believed to be on high mountain tops. There is a waterfall, formed by the River Liffey, in the Wicklow Mountains known as the Poula Phouk (the pooka's hole), and Binlaughlin Mountain in County Fermanagh is also known as the "peak of the speaking horse."

In some areas of the country, the pooka is rather more mysterious than dangerous, provided it is treated with proper respect. The pooka may even be helpful, on occasion, issuing prophecies and warnings where appropriate.

Only one man has ever managed to ride the pooka and that was Brian Boru, the High King of Ireland. Using a special bridle containing three hairs from the pooka's tail, Brian managed to control the magic horse and stay on its back until, exhausted, it surrendered to his will. The king extracted two promises from it; firstly, that it would no longer torment Christian people and ruin their property and, secondly, that it would never again attack an Irishman (all other nationalities are exempt), except those who are drunk or abroad with evil intent; the latter it could attack with greater ferocity than before. The pooka agreed to these conditions, but over the intervening years seems to have forgotten its bargain and attacks on property and sober travelers continue to this day.

THE SELKIE

Selkies are legendary creatures that appear in Irish, Scottish and Icelandic folklore. Generally they are imagined as seals that can transform themselves into human forms, usually those of beautiful women. It is thought that they achieve this by removing their seal skins, and that they return to being selkies by putting their skins back on again. *Selch* means "seal" in the dialect of Scotland's Orkney Islands.

The majority of tales about selkies feature a lonely fisherman who steals the selkie's seal skin while she is in human form, forcing her to come home with him and be his wife. In time, the couple will have children which may sometimes have webbed hands or other abnormalities; all the while, however, the selkie will continue to search for her skin, being unable to return to the sea without it. If found, the selkie will be unable to resist the lure of the sea, leaving her husband alone and desolate. In some cases, however, the man may remain completely unaware of his wife's true nature and may never know why she has seemingly disappeared forever.

Another legend says that if a lonely fisherman's wife drops seven tears into the sea, a merman will appear and make love to her.

OPPOSITE: The selkie removes her seal skin to appear as a beautiful woman.

124

CHAPTER FIVE
IRISH TALES & FAIRY FOLKLORE

THE HORNED WOMEN

In the Lower Shannon, on a large farm, there once lived a prosperous farmer with his family and his servants. Late one night, his wife, being unable to sleep, sat down to sew and as she did so heard a knock on the door.

"Open the door," a voice called out, to which the wife replied, "Who is there?" The voice said, "I am the witch of one horn." Curious, the wife opened the door and in came a woman with one large horn on her forehead and a pair of wool-carders in her hand. The horned woman sat herself down and began to card her wool and while doing so asked, "Where be my sisters for they tarry too long?"

Not five minutes had passed when there was another knock at the door and, obliged to answer it, the wife opened the door. There now entered another woman, this one with two horns coming from her forehead. "I am the witch of two horns," the woman said upon entering. In her hand she held a spinning wheel and, sitting down, began to spin as fast as the wind.

In the course of the next hour there would be more knocks upon the door, and with each knock would come another witch, each with one more horn than the one before, until the last one entered with 13 horns on her brow.

The witches all wove, producing a large cloth while they sang in an ancient tongue. Then the first to enter commanded the wife to bake them a cake, made with the blood of her family. By now the wife was completely in thrall to these dark entities and could do nothing but obey.

The wife, beset with grief, searched for a bucket in which to draw water for the cake. Her

sad expression became one of relief, however, when she could find no bucket, and no water meant no cake and no cake meant that her family would be spared.

The witches, however, bade her take a sieve and draw water in it, but when the wife came to the well and tried to do so the water poured through it. The wife didn't know what to do and began to sob, but a voice coming from the well called out, "Take yellow clay and moss and bind them together, using it to plaster the sieve and make it hold." The wife obeyed and the voice continued, "Go back to the house and when you approach its north side, cry out three times, 'The mountain of the Fenian women and the sky above it is all on fire!'"

The wife did as the voice commanded, and the witches immediately began to scream in terror as they flew away toward Slievenamon. Once they had disappeared, the spirit of the well spoke to the wife again: "Quickly now, we must prepare your house before their return."

The spirit commanded the wife to take water in which she had bathed the feet of her youngest child, and pour it onto the threshold of the door of the house. Next, she was instructed to take the cake, which in her absence the witches had made of meal, mixed with blood drawn from the bodies of the sleeping family, and place a morsel of the cake into each of their mouths, when the family would be restored to health.

The wife then took the cloth, which the witches had woven, and placed it half in and half out of the chest, locking the chest with the padlock. She then secured the door, fixing a great crossbeam across the jambs so that the witches could not enter. Having done all these things the wife waited.

The witches were enraged that the wife had duped them and demanded that the door be opened. But the door was fastened shut and they could not cross the feet-water poured across the threshold, even if they could have got the door to open.

The horned women screamed curses at the spirit of the well but to no avail, since the sun was soon to rise and they knew that their time was short.

The wife kept the witches' cloth and hung it beside the door as a reminder to be more careful, in the future, about letting strangers into the house.

THE WHITSUNTIDE LEGEND OF THE FAIRY HORSES

There was once a widow, with one son, who had a profitable farm of her own close to a lake. She took great care, when it came to cultivating her land, and her corn was the finest in the whole country. But every night, when the corn was near ready for cutting, she found it had been trampled down and all but destroyed, yet no one could tell who had done the deed.

So the widow set her son to watch. When midnight came, the son heard a great rushing of the water, and up out of the lake came a great herd of horses, which began to graze the corn, all the while trampling it down madly with their hoofs. The son recounted all this to his mother, and she instructed him to watch again the following night, and to take with him several of the farm hands, equipped with bridles which, when the horses rose from the lake, they were to fling over as many as they could catch.

The second night, the same great noise and rush of water was heard, and in an instant the field was filled with the fairy horses, grazing the corn and trampling it down. The men pursued the horses, but only succeeded in capturing one, albeit the noblest of them all, while the rest plunged back into the lake. The men brought home the captured horse, stabled it and cared for it, where it grew big and strong. But when a year had passed, and nothing more had been seen or heard, the widow began to think it a shame to keep so fine a horse idle, and she bade her son to take it out on the

Whitsuntide hunt that was to be attended by all the local gentry.

The horse acquitted itself well on the hunt, and every one admired the fine young rider as well as his handsome steed. But after the hunt, on the return home and on coming within sight of the lake, from which the fairy steed had risen, the horse began to plunge violently, and finally threw its rider. Tragically, the young man's foot was left caught in the stirrup, and he was dragged along while the horse continued its mad gallop to the lake, leaving fragments of the unhappy lad behind it on the road. On reaching the margin of the lake, the horse shook off what remained of the dead youth's body and, plunging into the waves, disappeared from sight.

The people reverently gathered up the remains of the dead boy, and erected a monument of stones over him in a field by the edge of the lake; and every one that passes by still lays a stone and says a prayer that the spirit of the dead boy may rest in peace.

The phantom horses were never seen again, but the lake has retained its evil reputation even to this day among the local people. No one would now venture in a boat upon the lake after sundown at Whitsuntide, or during the time of the ripening of the corn, or when the harvest was ready for the sickle, for strange sounds are to be heard at night, like the wild galloping of a horse across the meadow, along with the cries as of a man in his death agony.

THE STOLEN BRIDE

A fine young man was living at a place called Querin, in County Clare, in around 1670. He was brave and strong and rich, for he had his own land and his own house and was very much his own man. He was called the Kern of Querin, and it was his habit to go out alone at night to shoot wild fowl.

One cold frosty November Eve (Hallowe'en), he was watching for the wild geese, crouched down behind the ruins of an old hut, when a loud splashing sound attracted his attention. So he waited in silence for the approach of his victims.

Presently, he saw a dark mass moving along the edge of the beach, a mass that he knew instinctively was something other than the expected geese. So he watched and waited until the black mass drew nearer, when he perceived four stout men, carrying a bier on their shoulders, on which lay a corpse covered with a white cloth. For a few moments they laid it down, apparently to rest themselves, and the Kern instantly fired his gun, at which the four men ran away, shrieking, and the corpse was left alone on its bier. The Kern of Querin immediately ran to it, and lifting the cloth from the face of the corpse saw, by the cold light of the moon, that it was a beautiful young girl, who seemed to be sleeping rather than dead.

The Kern passed his hand gently over her face and raised her up, when she opened her eyes and looked around with wild wonderment. She uttered not a word, however, though he tried to soothe and encourage her. Then, thinking it was dangerous for them to remain in that place, he raised her from the bier and, taking her hand, led her away to his own house, where they arrived safely but in silence. For 12 months the girl remained with the Kern, neither tasting food nor speaking a word during all that time.

When the next November Eve came around, the Kern resolved to revisit the same part of the beach in the hope that something would happen that would throw light on the mystery of the beautiful girl. His way lay beside the old ruined Lios-na-Fallainge (the Fort of the Mantle), and as he passed, the sound of music and laughter could be heard. The Kern tried to catch what was being said and heard a man ask, in a low whisper, "Where shall we go tonight to carry off a bride?" And a second voice replied, "Wherever we go I hope better luck will be ours than we had this day twelve months ago."

"Yes," said a third, "on that night we carried off a rich prize, the fair daughter of O'Connor; but that clown, the Kern of Querin, broke our spell and took her from us. Yet little pleasure has he had of his bride, for she has neither eaten nor drunk nor uttered a word since she entered his house."

"And so she will remain," said a fourth, "until he makes her eat off her father's tablecloth, which covered her as she lay on the bier, and which is now thrown up over the top of her bed."

On hearing this, the Kern rushed home, and without even waiting for morning, entered the young girl's room, took down the tablecloth, spread it on the table, laid out meat and drink, and led her to it. "Drink," he said, "that speech may come to you." And she drank and ate and then speech came. And she told the Kern her story, how she was to have been married to a young lord of her own country, and the wedding guests had all assembled when she felt herself suddenly ill and swooned away, and never knew more of what had happened to her until the Kern had passed his hand over her face, by which time she had recovered consciousness but could neither eat nor speak, for a spell was on her and she was helpless.

Then the Kern prepared a chariot, and carried the young girl home to her father, who could not believe his eyes, thinking he had lost her forever. It was hardly surprising, then, when O'Connor, in gratitude, gave the Kern his fair young daughter to wife, following which the wedded pair lived happily together for many long years, and many good works were done in their names.

This story of the Kern of Querin still lingers in the Irish imagination, and is often retold by the peasants of Clare as they gather around the fire on November Eve, when the dead walk and the spirits of earth and air have power over mortals.

CATHAL MAC FINGUINE

Irish tradition has it that if the roots of the elder tree and the roots of an apple tree that bears red apples are boiled together and the potion drunk fasting, any evil that may have taken up residence in the body of a man will be expelled. But an evil charm to produce a living thing in the body can also be made by pronouncing a certain magic spell over the food or drink taken by any person that an enemy wishes to injure.

One should, therefore, be very cautious in accepting anything to eat from a malicious or spiteful person, or from anyone else who may wish one ill.

Cathal, King of Munster, was the tallest and most handsome of all the kings of Erin, and he fell deeply in love with the beautiful sister of Fergus, King of Ulster. The lovers resolved to marry, but Fergus, King of the North, had a mortal hatred to Cathal, King of the South, and secretly decided to prevent the marriage. So he set a watch over his sister, and by this means discovered that she was about to send a basket of the choicest apples to her lover by the hands of a trusty messenger. But before they could be delivered, Fergus managed to change the apples for some others, over which he had cast an evil spell. The substituted fruit was duly presented to Cathal, who, delighted at receiving this token of love from his princess, began at once to eat the apples. But the more he ate, the more he longed for, for a wicked spell had been placed on every one. When Cathal had at last eaten all the apples in the basket, he was compelled to send out for more, and he ate and ate until no apples remained, either in Cashel or in the country as a whole.

Then Cathal bade his chieftains go forth and bring in more food to appease his prodigious appetite; and he ate up all the cattle and the grain and the fruit, and still called for more, until the people were in great despair, for they had no more food and starvation was threatening all.

Now a great and wise man, the chief poet of his tribe, happened to be traveling through Munster at that time, and, hearing of the king's state, greatly desired to see him, for he recognized the devil's work when he saw it. Having been brought into the presence of the king, the wise man uttered many powerful incantations, for poets have a knowledge of mysteries above all other men; finally, after three days had passed, the poet announced to the lords and chiefs that on that night, when the moon rose, the spell would be broken and the king restored to his usual good health. All the chiefs gathered in the courtyard to watch, but no one was allowed to enter the room where the king lay, save the poet, who was to give the signal when the hour had come and the spell would be broken.

As they watched, and just as the moon rose, a great cry was heard coming from the king's room, and the poet, flinging open the door, bade the chiefs enter. There on the floor lay a huge dead wolf, which, for a whole year, had taken up his abode in the king's body but was now happily cast out by the powerful incantations of the poet.

After this, the king fell into a deep sleep, and when he arose he was quite well and, as ever, in all the pride and beauty of his youth. At this, the people greatly rejoiced, for he was greatly loved, and the poet who had restored him was honored above all men in the land; the king himself took off the golden torque that encircled his own neck, and placed it on that of the poet, setting him at his right hand at the feast.

Now a strange thing happened at about the same time; Fergus, King of the North, suddenly fell ill, wasting away to a shadow of his former self. He died, before a year had passed, when Cathal the king wedded his beloved princess, and they lived happily ever after.

OPPOSITE: The Rock of Cashel was the stronghold of Cathal mac Finguine, King of Munster, who belonged to the dominant Eóganachta kin-group whose members dominated Munster from the 7th–10th centuries.

BEWITCHED BUTTER

A wealthy farmer, named Brian Costigan, once kept an extensive farm with a great many dairy cows. The excellence of his pasture ensured that Brian's cows were the healthiest and most productive in the country. Consequently, his milk and butter was the richest and sweetest and the most sought after in every marketplace.

For many years Brian prospered until, one season, everything on the farm began to go wrong. At first, Brian attributed this change in his fortunes to the weather, or some such cause, but soon found reasons to believe that something more sinister was afoot. The cows, though outwardly still healthy-looking, began daily to deteriorate and, despite all the good grass, began to lose weight; what little milk the cows were still able to produce, moreover, was so bitter that even the pigs would not drink it.

Brian began to look for remedies, seeking the advice of quacks and "fairy women" but to no avail. Many declared the mysterious malady to be beyond their power to cure; while others, although they found no difficulty in attributing the troubles to supernatural activity, felt unable to suggest a remedy. The poor farmer was now staring ruin in the face; he could not even sell his cattle and purchase others, for no one would buy them in their present state.

One sultry evening in late July, when Brian's wife was sitting at her door, spinning at her wheel in a very depressed and agitated state of mind, she happened to glance down the narrow green lane, which led to her cabin, when she saw a little old woman, walking barefoot and enveloped in an old scarlet cloak, approaching slowly with the aid of a crutch, which she supported with one hand, and with a cane or walking-stick in the other. Brian's wife felt oddly hopeful at seeing the stranger; she even suppressed a smiled, though she knew not why, as the old woman neared the house, bidding her welcome to her house with uncharacteristic warmth.

Brian's wife ran and placed a chair near to the fire, but the old woman refused it, sitting on the floor instead. Mrs. Costigan was now able to examine the old hag more closely. The woman appeared to be of a great age and was extremely ugly, even repulsive; her skin was rough and weatherbeaten, her forehead low, narrow and covered in a thousand wrinkles; her long gray hair fell in matted locks from beneath a white linen skull-cap; her eyes were bloodshot and deep-set; her voice was croaky, tremulous and, at times, difficult to understand. As she squatted on the floor, the visitor looked about her inquisitively, rudely peering into every corner and

taking stock of all the Costigans' possessions. Mrs. Costigan continued to watch her strange visitor with mingled curiosity and pleasure.

"Are you not the owner of the cattle I see yonder?" asked the old hag.

Mrs. Costigan replied in the affirmative, and briefly related to her the circumstances of their misfortunes. Meanwhile, the old woman remained silent, but shook her gray head repeatedly as she continued to gaze about the room.

As Mrs. Costigan finished her sorry tale, the old hag remained in deep thought: at length she asked, "Have you any of the milk in the house?" "I have," replied the other. "Show me some of it." A jug was filled from a vessel and was handed to the old woman, who smelt it, then tasted it, and spat out what milk she had taken onto the floor. "Where is your husband?" she asked. "Out in the fields," was the reply. "I must see him."

A messenger was sent for Brian, who presently made an appearance. "Neighbor," said the stranger, "your wife informs me that your cattle are sick."

"She informs you right," said Brian. "And why have you not sought a cure?" "A cure!" repeated the man. "Why, woman, I have sought cures until I am heartbroken, and all in vain; they get worse every day."

"What will you give me if I cure them for you?" "Anything in our power," replied Brian and his wife, speaking with one accord. "All I will ask from you is a silver coin, and that you will do everything that I will bid you," said the hag.

The farmer and his wife seemed astonished at the moderation of her demand and offered her substantially more.

"No," said the old woman, "I don't want your money; I am no cheat, and I would not even take a penny but that I can do nothing until I handle some of your silver."

The coin was immediately handed over, and complete obedience was promised by both Brian and his wife, who had begun to regard the old woman as something of a godsend.

The hag pulled off the black silken ribbon which encircled her head inside her cap, and gave it to Brian, saying, "Go, now, and the first cow you touch with this ribbon, turn her into the yard, but be sure not to touch the second, nor speak a word until you return; also be careful not to let the ribbon touch the ground for all is over if you do."

Brian took the ribbon, and soon returned, driving a red cow before him.

The old hag went out and, approaching the cow, began to pull hairs out of its tail, while intoning a strange, wild song. The cow appeared

restive and uneasy, but the old witch continued her mysterious chant until she had extracted nine hairs. She then ordered the cow to be driven back to her pasture, when she again entered the house.

"Go, now," said she to Brian's wife, "and bring me some milk from every cow in your possession."

Mrs. Costigan went and returned with a large pail of milk. The old woman poured it into the churn.

"Now," she said, "you both must churn; make fast the door and windows, and let there be no light but from the fire; do not open your lips until I tell you, and by observing my directions we will discover the infernal villain who is robbing you."

Brian secured the doors and windows and commenced churning. The old sorceress sat down by a blazing fire, specially lit for the occasion, and began to intone the same wild song as before, after a while casting one of the nine hairs into the fire.

A loud cry, as if from a female in distress, was now heard coming from outside the house; the old witch discontinued her incantations, listening attentively. The crying came nearer to the door.

"Open the door quickly," shouted the witch.

Brian unbarred the door, and all three rushed out into the yard, where they heard the same cry but could see nothing.

"It is all over," shouted the old witch; "something has gone amiss and our charm is, for the present, ineffectual."

As they re-entered, crestfallen, the witch caught sight of a horseshoe nailed to the threshold, leading her to exclaim, "Here I have it; no wonder our charm was abortive. The person that was crying abroad is the villain who has bewitched your cattle; I brought her to the house, but she was not able to enter on account of that horseshoe. Remove it instantly, and we will try our luck again."

Brian removed the horseshoe and, at the hag's direction, placed it on the floor beneath the churn, having previously reddened the horseshoe in the fire. Brian and his wife again began to churn, and the witch continued with her strange incantations, casting her cow-hairs into the fire. The old woman was by now looking vexed and disappointed. She had grown quite pale, and was gnashing her teeth; her hand trembled as she cast the ninth and last hair into the fire.

Once more the cry was heard, and an aged red-haired woman was seen approaching the house. "Ho, ho!" roared the witch. "I knew it would be so; my charm has succeeded; my expectations are realized, and here she comes, the villain who has destroyed you."

"What are we to do now?" asked Brian. "Say nothing to her," said the hag; "give her whatever she demands and leave the rest to me."

The woman advanced, still screeching, and Brian went out to meet her. She said she was a neighbor, and that one of her best cows was drowning in a pool of water. She implored Brian to go rescue the cow, there being no one at home but herself. Brian accompanied her without hesitation and, having saved the cow, was back again within a quarter of an hour.

LEFT & OPPOSITE: In this tale the Costigans' butter, when churned, was tainted.

It was now sunset, and Mrs. Costigan set about preparing supper, during which time the singular events of the day were discussed. The old witch uttered many a cackling laugh at the success of her magic, and asked for the identity of the red-haired woman to be disclosed.

Brian satisfied her in every particular. She was the wife of a neighboring farmer; her name was Rachel Higgins, and she had long been suspected of being on familiar terms with the spirits of darkness. She had five or six cows; but it had been observed by her neighbors that she sold more butter every year than others who had 20. Brian had had his suspicions about her for some time, but being without proof he had held his peace.

"Well," said the old witch, with a grim smile, "it is not enough that we have merely discovered the robber; all is in vain if we do not take steps to punish her for the past as well as preventing her mischief-making in the future." "And how will that be done?" said Brian.

"I will tell you; as soon as the hour of 12 o'clock arrives tonight, go to the pasture and take a couple of swift-running dogs with you; conceal yourself in some place convenient to the cattle; watch them carefully, and if you see anything, whether it be man or beast, approach the cows, set the dogs on them, and if possible make them draw the blood of the intruder; then all will be accomplished. If nothing approaches before sunrise, you may return, and we will try something else."

Conveniently to hand lived the cowherd of a neighboring squire. He was a hardy, courageous young man, and kept a pair of ferocious bulldogs. Brian asked for assistance, and the cowherd cheerfully agreed to accompany him. He also proposed to fetch a couple of his master's best greyhounds, as his own dogs, although fierce and bloodthirsty, could not be relied upon for swiftness. He promised Brian to be with him before 12 o'clock, and the two took their leave.

Brian stayed awake that night, sitting up anxiously awaiting the midnight hour when the herdsman, true to his promise, arrived. After further instructions from the old woman, the two departed and, arriving at the field, concealed themselves and waited, the four dogs lying beside them.

Brian and his comrade were getting impatient as dawn approached, and were thinking of returning home when there was a rushing sound behind them and they perceived a large hare in the act of springing from the ditch. They were now convinced that this was what they had been waiting for, and were resolved to watch the creature closely.

Having arrived in the field, the hare remained motionless for a few moments, then began to skip and jump in a playful manner, advancing at a smart pace toward the cows. It began to suckle each cow in turn, frightening them and making them agitated. Brian could hardly restrain himself, but his wiser companion suggested it was better to wait until the hare was satisfied, when it would be much heavier and less able to escape. This proved to be true, for now the hare's belly was enormously distended, and it was moving more slowly and with difficulty in its advance toward the ditch where it had entered. As it approached the spot where the two men were crouched, the pair started up and the hare took off, the dogs in mad pursuit.

Rachel Higgins' cabin appeared through the gray morning mist, and it was evident that the hare had been heading for it all along, despite having made a detour to throw off its pursuers. Brian and his comrade, however, suddenly arrived as the hare, panting and exhausted, ran around the house, evidently confused. In the bottom of the front door was a small, semi-circular aperture, that permitted a cat to enter and leave. The hare now made a last and desperate effort, and had succeeded in forcing its head and shoulders through the aperture when one of the dogs seized it violently by the haunch. The hare uttered a piercing scream as it struggled desperately to free itself, and at last succeeded in getting into the house.

The men burst open the door and beheld a bright turf fire blazing on the hearth. The floor was streaming with blood, but of the hare, however, there was no sign.

The two men entered the adjacent bedroom, and there, beneath a bundle of freshly-cut rushes, they discovered Rachel Higgins, writhing in the most excruciating agony and smothered in blood. The men were astounded; they addressed the wretched woman, but either she could not or would not answer them. At length she expired.

Brian and his friend returned home. The old hag seemed already aware of the fate of Rachel Higgins and was delighted at the outcome of her mysterious machinations. Brian pressed her to accept some remuneration for her services, which she promptly refused. She remained a few days at the Costigans' house, and at length took her leave and departed, no one knew whither.

Old Rachel's remains were interred in the local churchyard. The story, however, endures in the memory of the villagers. Often, it is said, amid the grey haze of a summer twilight, the ghost of Rachel Higgins, in the form of a hare, may be seen in the vicinity of the cabin where she once lived.

BELOW: The ghost of Rachel Higgins appears in the form of a hare.

THE FAIRY RATH

The ruins of ancient raths or compounds are still thought to be ruled by the Sidhe race, and there are many superstitions connected with walking over the remains of old ring forts and lisses (court-yards), as it was thought that misfortune would befall anyone who disturbed the Sidhe's peace. There are also accounts of people becoming inexplicably lost after walking over the site of an ancient ring fort.

The fairies, beside being vengeful are also very arrogant, and will allow no interference with what they consider to be their long-established rights.

There is a rath in County Laois, only four yards in diameter, but it is held to be so sacred as the fairies' dancing-ground, that no one dares to remove a handful of earth from the mound. At night, the sweetest music, played on silver bagpipes, may be heard floating softly through the air.

BELOW: An ancient Iron-Age fort, with interior enclosures, near Coomakista Pass on the Ring of Kerry.

OPPOSITE ABOVE: A Fairy Ring, by Walter Jenks Morgan (1847–1924).

OPPOSITE BELOW: Dun Eochla is a ring fort located at the highest point on Inishmore, the largest of the Aran Islands, having been built some time between AD 550 and 800.

One evening a boy lay down on the rath to listen to the fairy music and, without thinking, began to gather up balls of clay from the mound, carelessly flinging them here and there, when suddenly he was struck down by a violent blow and knocked senseless.

He was eventually found by people who had been searching for him and, when he came to himself, he was bleating like a calf. It was a long time before he recovered his reason, for the power of the fairies is said to be potent, and no one is able to resist it.

THE FAIRY PATH

According to folklore, a fairy path is a route habitually followed by fairies. It usually proceeds in a straight line and links sites of traditional significance, such as fairy forts or raths (circular earthworks dating from the Iron Age), mountains and hills, thorn bushes, springs, lakes, rocky outcrops, and Stone Age monuments. Ley lines and spirit paths, such as corpse roads, share some similarities with these fairy pathways.

In Ireland, people who were sick or otherwise unfortunate were suspected of living in houses that were "in the way" or in a "contrary place," meaning they were obstructing a fairy path, an example being that of a family in which four children became sick and died, leaving the doctors baffled as to the cause. A fifth child also became sick and was near to death when it made a sudden and full recovery. The father told the doctor that he had consulted a wise woman who had informed him that his new house, recently extended, blocked a fairy path between two fairy forts, whereupon he demolished it and the child regained its health.

Another example of the straightness of a fairy path appears in an account concerning a croft (now a cattle shed) at Knockeencreen, Brosna, County Kerry. In the 1980s, the last human occupant of the croft told of the troubles his grandfather had experienced with his cattle periodically and inexplicably dying. The front door was exactly opposite the back door, and the grandfather had been informed by a passing gypsy that the dwelling stood on a fairy path running between two hills. The gypsy advised the man to keep the doors slightly ajar at night to allow the fairies free passage through. The advice was heeded and the problem was solved. It so happens that the building, besides being on a straight line drawn between two local hilltops, is also at one end of a long, straight track.

It was said that the fairies processed from Rath Ringlestown every night, and that parents brought their children indoors before the fairies were due to pass. The path passed around several bushes which were left undisturbed by the locals after a man, who had cut one of the bushes down, could not get it to burn and who himself sickened and died within a short time. The route also passed between two mud-walled houses and a man who was outside at the wrong time was found dead, the fairies having taken him for getting in the way of their procession.

Some builders used a technique to see if a planned construction was going to be on a fairy path; they would map out the floor plan in the earth and place a pile of stones at each corner, leaving them overnight. If the stones were undisturbed, then it was safe to build, otherwise the work could not continue. Builders were also advised against using white quartz in their stonework, as it was said to be a fairy stone.

LEFT: Fairy pathways often follow ley lines connecting stone circles and raths.

OPPOSITE: An artist's impression of a fairy path.

CHAPTER SIX

ANCIENT & SACRED SITES

THE HILL OF TARA

The Hill of Tara, known as *Teamhair* in Gaelic, was once the ancient seat of power in Ireland, and 142 kings are said to have reigned there in prehistoric and historic times. According to ancient Irish religion and mythology, Tara was the sacred place or dwelling of the gods and the entrance to the Otherworld. St. Patrick is said to have come to Tara to challenge the religious beliefs of the pagans at this their most powerful site.

One interpretation of the name Tara is as a "place of great prospect" and indeed, on a clear day, it is claimed that features of half the counties of Ireland can be seen from its summit. In the distance, to the northwest, is visible the brilliant

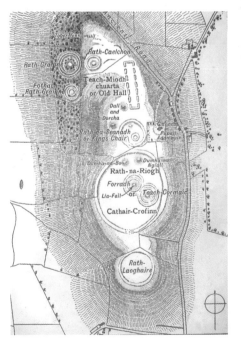

white quartz front of Newgrange, a prehistoric monument located in County Meath, and further north the Hill of Slane where, according to legend, St. Patrick lit his Pascal fire prior to his mission of conversion to Tara in AD 433.

LEFT: An old plan of the Hill of Tara, showing the full extent of the site.

ABOVE: The Stone of Destiny (Lia Fáil), where the High Kings of Ireland were crowned.

OPPOSITE: The Banqueting Hall earthwork.

The most important of the many earthworks at Tara are to be found on the summit of the hill inside an enclosure called Ráth na Ríogh (the Fort of the Kings or Royal Enclosure), dating from the Iron Age in the first five centuries AD. The axis of the oval enclosure measures 1,043ft (318m) from north to south and by 866ft (264m) east to west. The ring-shaped formations within this enclosure are known as Cormac's House (Teach Chormaic) and the Royal Seat or Forradh. In the middle of the Forradh is a standing stone, believed to be the Lia Fáil (the Stone of Destiny), at which the High Kings of Ireland were crowned. According to legend, the stone let out a screech that could be heard all over Ireland, when a series of challenges were met by the would-be king. To the north, just outside the boundaries of the Ráth na Riog, is a ring fort with three banks, known as the Rath of the Synods (Ráth na Seanadh). Excavations of this monument have produced Roman artifacts dating from the 1st–3rd centuries AD.

Further north is a long, narrow rectangular feature, known as the Banqueting Hall (Teach Miodhchuarta), where the legendary High King (*Ard Ri*) feasted, dating back either to the Bronze or Iron Age. This was possibly the ceremonial entrance

onto Tara, where the roads to the hill met. It is aligned with the Neolithic Duma na nGiall.

To the south of the Ráth na Ríogh or Royal Enclosure lies a ring fort known as Ráth Lóegaire or Lóegaire's (Laoghaire's) Fort, where the eponymous king is said to have been buried in an upright position. Half a mile south of the Hill of Tara is another hill fort called Rath Maeve, the fort either of the legendary Queen Medb, who is more usually associated with Connacht, or the less well-known mythical figure of Medb Lethderg, associated with Tara.

Historians have been working for centuries to uncover Tara's mysteries, and have suggested that, from the time of the first Gaelic influence until the 1169 invasion of Richard de Clare (Strongbow), the Hill of Tara was Ireland's political and spiritual

ABOVE: The megalithic passage tomb called the Mound of the Hostages (Duma na nGiall) is the oldest monument on the Hill of Tara, dating back to between 2500 and 3000 BC. The passage is subdivided into three compartments, each one containing cremated remains.

RIGHT: A view from Tara of the Boyne valley beyond.

146

capital; recent research, however, suggests that the complete story of the wider area around the Hill of Tara is yet to be revealed.

It is believed that the Hill of Tara's primary role was as the seat of the High Kings of Ireland until the 6th century – a role that extended until the 12th century, albeit with none of the splendor of the earlier period. The significance of the Hill of Tara, however, predates Celtic times, although it has not been shown that Tara had been continuously important from the Neolithic Age to the 12th century. The central part of the site could not have housed a large permanent retinue, suggesting that it was used as an occasional meeting place and that there were no large defensive works. Certainly the earliest records confirm that High Kings were inaugurated here, and the Seanchas Mor legal text (written down after AD 600) specified that they had to drink ale and symbolically marry the goddess Medb to acquire this important office.

The case for Tara's importance advanced as archeologists identified pre-Celtic monuments and buildings, dating back to the Neolithic period around 5,000 years ago. To the north of the ring forts is a small Neolithic passage tomb, known as Duma na nGiall (the Mound of the Hostages), which was constructed in around 3,400 BC, the tomb being similar in layout to those at nearby Newgrange and Knowth but on a much smaller scale. The short passage is astronomically aligned (less accurately than some) with the sunrises on February 4 and November 8, which is around the time of the ancient Celtic festivals of Imbolc and Samhain. Just inside the passage on the left is a carved stone, while several Bronze Age burials were excavated in the tomb itself.

A theory that may predate the Hill of Tara's importance before Celtic times is the legend naming Tara as the capital of the Tuatha Dé Danann, the pre-Celtic dwellers of Ireland. When the Celts established a seat on the hill, Tara became the place from which the Kings of Mide ruled Ireland. There is much debate among historians as to how far the kings' influence spread; it may have been as little as

OPPOSITE & ABOVE: St. Patrick's influence on Tara is plain to see, with a statue of him and a church that bears his name. The churchyard also contains two standing stones, these being remnants of ancient Tara, which Patrick visited while on his mission to convert the pagan High King Lóegaire, and his subjects, to Christianity.

the middle of Ireland, or may have been the whole of the northern half. The High Kingship of the whole island was only established to an effective degree by Máel Sechnaill mac Máele Ruanaid (Malachy I), although Irish pseudohistorians of the Middle Ages claim it stretched back into prehistoric times.

In the churchyard at Tara are two standing stones which are believed to be ancient – remnants of a time when there were many stone monuments on Tara. The taller of the two is thought to be a figure of the Celtic fertility god, Cernunnos, and is similar to many of the *Sheela na Gig* (figurative carvings of naked women) found across Ireland. These stones may date to the Neolithic period but are more likely to have had their origin in the Bronze Age.

RIGHT: Tara is at its most mysterious and enigmatic at sunset.

NAVAN FORT (EMAIN MACHA)

Navan Fort, known in Old Irish as Emain Macha, is an ancient monument in County Armagh, in Ulster, and, according to Irish legend, was one of the major power centers of pre-Christian Ireland. The site that can be seen today is little more than a grass-covered mound, but according to the *Oxford Dictionary of Celtic Mythology*, "... the Emain Macha of myth and legend is a far grander and mysterious place than archeological excavation supports."

Although referred to as a "fort," Emain Macha is more likely to have been a pagan ritual or ceremonial site, and is often regarded as the traditional capital of the Ulaidh (Ulster). It also features prominently in Irish mythology, particularly in the tales of the Ulster Cycle.

The site comprises a circular enclosure 820ft (250m) in diameter, surrounded by a bank and ditch. Unusually, the ditch is inside the bank, suggesting it was not built for defensive purposes. Inside the enclosure two monuments are visible: off-center to the northwest is an earthen mound 130ft (40m) in diameter and 20ft (6m) high. Also slightly off-center to the southeast is the circular impression of a ring barrow, the plowed-down remains of a late-prehistoric ceremonial or burial monument, about 100ft (30m) in diameter.

Archeological excavations have revealed that the construction of the 130-ft mound dates to 95 BC (dated by dendrochronology). A circular structure, consisting of four concentric rings of posts around a central oak trunk, was built with its entrance facing west (prehistoric houses invariably faced east, toward the sunrise). The floor of the building was covered with stones arranged in radiating segments, and the whole edifice was deliberately burnt down before being covered in a mound of earth and turf (there is archeological evidence for similar repeated construction and immolation of Tara and Dún Ailinne). The bank and ditch that surround the hilltop were built at the same time.

No precise date can be assigned to the ring barrow, but excavations and geophysical surveys have revealed the remains of a figure-of-eight-

shaped wooden building beneath. The larger ring of the figure-of-eight is 100ft (30m) in diameter, the smaller about 65ft (20m). The building was rebuilt twice. Similar, slightly smaller structures, each with central hearths, were found under the 130-ft mound, and artifacts found in these layers show

they were inhabited in the late Bronze Age and early Iron Age (approximately 600 to at least 250 BC). Perhaps the most unusual item found in these layers was the skull of a Barbary macaque.

An earlier Bronze Age structure, a circular ditch surrounding the mound, 150ft (45m) in diameter, 16ft (5m) wide and 3ft (1m) deep, was also found, and flint tools and fragments of pottery show activity at the site in the Neolithic period (ca. 4000–2500 BC).

ABOVE: Navan Fort.

THE ROCK OF CASHEL

Legend associates the Rock of Cashel with St. Patrick, but the name comes from *caiseal*, meaning "stone fort," the hill originally having been the residence of the kings of Munster. Excavations have revealed some evidence of burials and church buildings from the 9th or 10th centuries, but it was in the early 12th century that the rock came to be developed into a major Christian center.

In 1101, Muircheartach Ua Briain, King of Munster, gave the Rock of Cashel to the church. A round tower, which still stands today, was erected shortly after this, and a decade later, in 1111, Cashel became the seat of an archbishop. (At the time there was only one other archbishop in Ireland, located in Armagh.) The original cathedral was located where the choir of the present one now stands, but nothing is known of it.

Cormac's Chapel, a magnificent little Romanesque church that survives to this day, was

BELOW, OPPOSITE & OVERLEAF: The Rock of Cashel is an imposing stucture which has recently undergone some restoration.

consecrated in 1134, probably for Benedictine monks. The town of Cashel, at the foot of the rock, was founded by the archbishop some time before 1218 and a Dominican priory was established in 1243. The present cathedral was also erected in the 13th century.

The frescoes in Cormac's Chapel, which are the oldest Romanesque wall paintings in Ireland, were covered with whitewash at the Reformation (16th-century) and remained hidden until the 1980s.

OPPOSITE: Many of the buildings are in ruins.

BELOW & OVERLEAF: The rock towers over the village of Cashel lying at its foot.

THE BLARNEY STONE

Five miles northwest of the small city of Cork is the village of Blarney, near to which, standing almost 90ft (27m) high, is the Castle of Blarney with its world-famous Blarney Stone. More than 300,000 people come to kiss the Blarney Stone each year, in the hope of acquiring eloquence and the "gift of the gab" (the word blarney has come to mean "clever, flattering or coaxing talk"). It is said that Queen Elizabeth I wanted the Irish chiefs to agree to occupy their own lands under title from her. Cormac Teige MacCarthy, the Lord of Blarney, handled every Royal request with subtle diplomacy, promising loyalty to the queen without actually "giving in." Elizabeth remarked that McCarthy was giving her "a lot of Blarney," thus giving rise to the popular legend.

ABOVE & BELOW: The safest way to kiss the Blarney Stone is to lay on one's back, with a friend sitting on one's legs.

OPPOSITE: Blarney Castle.

ANCIENT & SACRED SITES

While the Blarney Castle that visitors see today was constructed in 1446, the history of the place stretches back two centuries before that time. The story begins with a magical stone, its origins shrouded in mystery. One legend tells that it was the rock that Moses struck with his staff to produce water for the Israelites during their exodus from Egypt, while another says it was once

Jacob's pillow and that the prophet Jeremiah brought the stone to Ireland.

Some, however, believe it was the Stone of Ezel, which David hid behind on Jonathan's advice while fleeing from King Saul, and that it was brought to Ireland during the Crusades. Others even claim that it may once have been a half-portion of the Stone of Scone, the Coronation Stone of Scottish monarchs, and was later used by St. Columba as a traveling altar during his missionary activities throughout Scotland. After Columba's death it may have been brought to Ireland where it served as the Lia Fáil, or Stone of Destiny, and was used in the inauguration of the High Kings of Ireland.

Kissing the Blarney Stone was once a more difficult feat than it is today, in that people had to hang by their heels over the edge of the parapet. One day, however, a pilgrim slipped from the grasp of his friends and went hurtling down to certain death, since then another method has been adopted. First, the person sits with his back toward the stone, then another person sits on his legs or firmly holds his feet. Next, leaning far back and downward into the abyss, while grasping the iron rails, the person lowers himself until his head is level with the stone.

Just how long this custom has been practiced, or how it originated, is not known, but a local legend claims that an old woman, saved from drowning by a king of Munster, rewarded him with the promise of an eloquence that would captivate all if he kissed the stone.

LEFT: The castle originally dates from before AD 1200, when a wooden structure was believed to have been built on the site, although no evidence of this remains. This was replaced, in around 1210, by a stone fortification that was destroyed in 1446 but subsequently rebuilt by Cormac Laidir MacCarthy, Lord of Muscry (Muskerry).

NEWGRANGE

Along the River Boyne, north of Dublin, stands the Brú na Boínne (Palace of the Boyne), containing 26 extraordinary structures, of which Newgrange, Knowth and Dowth are the most significant. Newgrange is named after the local townland of Newgrange, so-called when the area was part of the Mellifont Cistercian abbey in the 12th century.

The complex of Newgrange was originally built between ca. 3100 and 2900 BC, which makes it approximately 5,000 years old, i.e., more than 500 years older than the Great Pyramid of Giza in Egypt. It also predates Stonehenge in England by about 1,000 years.

Legend tells that the area of these mounds was the home of Aengus, the son of Bóann and her

lover, the Dagda, and was known as the Mansion of Aengus, the area as a whole being the Brú na Boínne (Palace of the Boyne). According to another Celtic legend, the Dagda and his son Aengus were two of the principal members of the Tuatha Dé Danann, which therefore placed the mounds under the protection of the Sidhe. In 1699, the owner of the land, Charles Campbell, discovered the decorated stone at the entrance to Newgrange and became possibly the first person to enter the cairn in a millennium. Recognizing the importance of the structure, he stopped quarrying its stones and excavations began in 1962.

BELOW: Newgrange is by far the most impressive of the 26 structures making up the Brú na Boínne.

The Newgrange passage cairn covers an acre of land and consists of a mound, sometimes called a tumulus, rising from the meadow and surrounded by a stone curbing. The cairn is 280ft (85m) across and 50ft (15m) high; of the original 38 pillar stones surrounding the cairn, only 12 remain. The bulk of the cairn is constructed of approximately 280,000 tons of river-rolled granite stones, brought 75 miles (120km) from Dundalk Bay and covered with a layer of soil several yards deep. The facing around the perimeter of the cairn is several yards high and is made of sparkling white quartz quarried 50 miles (80km) away in the Wicklow Mountains. The entrance to the cairn is marked by a threshold stone which is elaborately carved with spirals and diamond shapes. Inside the cairn, a 62-ft (19-m) passageway leads to a domed chamber that is 20ft (6m) high. This chamber has a corbeled roof and three recesses, one straight ahead and one on either side, creating a cruciform shape. Many of the stones within these chambers are also richly decorated with beautiful spirals, geometric figures and wavy lines.

Above the main entrance to the cairn are two lintels and between them an opening, called a "roofbox," through which a beam of sunlight, on a particular sequence of days, is able to enter the long chamber. A fascinating fact is that the 62-ft passageway rises 6.5ft along its length, resulting in the chamber floor being level with the roofbox. One of the primary aims of those forms of megalithic architecture, which functioned as celestial observatories, was to reduce the light in the interior of the passage chamber; the darker the chamber, the more brilliant the narrow shaft of light would appear to be. Furthermore, the accuracy of such devices precisely to observe the sun increases in proportion to their size. Unless the construct is of an extremely large size, such as that to be found at Newgrange, the varying positions of

RIGHT Newgrange is surrounded by standing stones, some of which bear carvings indicating that their builders were astronomically aware.

the light beam will be almost undetectable during the 22-day period of the solstice.

Just before 9 am on the morning of the winter solstice, December 21, the Newgrange passage is pierced by a shaft of sunlight which illuminates a stone basin at the end of the passage and lights up a series of intricate spiral carvings in the rock. The chamber is brilliantly lit for around 17 minutes and this solar display lasts for five days around the time of the solstice.

Archeoastronomers studying the various cairns at Newgrange, Knowth and Dowth have determined that the sunbeam on the solstice is accurately observed throughout the day by the different cairns. Furthermore, standing stones and cairns in close proximity to the Newgrange

tumulus create sightlines which clearly indicate that the ancient builders were also precisely aware of other astronomically significant periods, such as the equinoxes, the cross-quarter days, and both major and minor lunar standstills. Even more fascinating is the fact that the scholars Christopher Knight and Robert Lomas have conclusively demonstrated that the precise alignment and engineering of the roofbox also indicated one day – occurring only every eight years – when the light of Venus enters the passage exactly 24 minutes before the light of the solstice sun.

OPPOSITE: The main entrance to Newgrange.

ABOVE: Detail of the entrance's spiral decoration.

The passage cairn of Newgrange (and others such as Knowth, Dowth and Loughcrew) has often been compared to a womb, as the inside of a great mound of earth may be likened to the womb of an earth goddess. This notion is supported by the fact that very few burial remains have been found within any of the large cairns of Ireland. What have been found, however, all seem to be connected with fertility, such as oval-shaped stones and rock phalluses. Some carved bone pins and pendants have also been recovered from the cairns and scholars suggest that these may have been left by

young women in the hope of being impregnated by the gods. The few bones found within the cairns, always without rich burial artifacts, may be an indication that the ancient people hoped the sun's rays would touch the bones and somehow allow the spirit within to reincarnate.

BELOW: The Newgrange complex is said to be the palace of mythical ancient kings.

KNOWTH

Knowth (Cnoghbha) is a Neolithic passage tomb and ancient monument of Brú na Bóinne, situated in the valley of the River Boyne in Ireland. It is the largest of all the passage tombs situated within the Brú na Bóinne complex.

The site consists of one large mound (known as Site 1) and 17 smaller satellite tombs. Knowth (Site 1) is essentially a large mound measuring about 40ft (12m) high and 220ft (67m) in diameter, covering roughly a hectare overall. It contains two passages, placed along an east to west line. It is encircled by 127 curbstones, three of which are missing and four badly damaged.

The large mound has been estimated to date from between 2500 and 2000 BC. The passages are independent of one another, and each leads to a burial chamber. The eastern passage leads to a cruciform chamber, not unlike that found at Newgrange. It contains three recesses and basin stones into which the cremated remains of the dead were placed.

The right-hand recess is larger and more elaborately decorated with megalithic art than the others, which is typical of Irish passage graves of this type, the reason for this being unknown. The western passage ends in an undifferentiated chamber, separated from the passage by a sill stone. The chamber seems also to have contained a basin stone. This was later removed and is now located about two-thirds down the passageway.

BELOW, OPPOSITE & OVERLEAF: The Knowth complex and interior of one of the mounds.

THE ROUND TOWERS OF IRELAND

Scattered seemingly at random across the rolling hills of Ireland are the remains of 65 round towers. Standing as much as 112ft (34m) above the ground, the towers are in remarkably fine condition considering their great age. When the towers were constructed is unknown, but it has been suggested that the most probable construction period was between the 7th and 10th centuries AD, based on the fact that nearly every tower is at the site of a known Celtic church dating from the 5th–12th centuries. Each of the towers were initially freestanding structures but in later times other buildings, primarily churches and monastic foundations, were constructed around some of them.

Thirteen towers retain conical caps and it is assumed that all the others once had similar ones that have fallen in over the centuries, while on a small number of them, battlements were added, possibly in the Middle Ages. The method of construction is always the same: two walls of block and mortar are built a few feet from one another and the space between filled in with rock rubble, in a standard method utilized by the Romans. Scholars believe that Christian missionaries learned the technique in England or in continental Europe, then brought the building technology to Ireland.

All the towers appear to follow a similar pattern and all are of a similar size and width. Doorways, windows, story heights and diameters also follow clearly defined patterns, and it is safe to assume that most of the towers were the work of teams of builders that moved from one monastery to another, utilizing standard designs.

RIGHT: The Kilree round tower, in County Kilkenny, has lost its conical cap.

OPPOSITE: The Ardmore round tower, in County Waterford, has three distinctive brick courses and a noticeable lean.

It had also been discovered that the seemingly random geographical arrangement of the round towers, throughout the Irish countryside, actually mirrors the positions of the stars in the northern sky during the time of the winter solstice.

Archeological excavations at the bases of the towers have also revealed that many of them were

OPPOSITE: Monasterboice round tower, in County Louth, forms part of an early Christian settlement.

ABOVE: Devenish is an island in Lower Lough Erne, County Fermanagh. Its round tower can be climbed.

RIGHT: Clondalkin, Dublin, is a well-preserved 8th-century round tower that acts as a focal point for the area. Acknowledged as one of the oldest and best preserved in the country, it is 84ft (26m) high and has its original conical cap.

erected over the tops of much older graves; it is also known that many of the tower sites were considered to be sacred places long before the arrival of Christianity in Ireland.

These facts lead us to wonder if the ancient Irish, like the Egyptians, the Mayans and many other archaic cultures, considered there to be an energetic resonance between specific terrestrial locations and different celestial bodies. This certainly seems to be the case, for all across the Irish countryside particular locations were chosen, precisely designed structures were erected to gather and store various energies, and a tradition of

human spiritual use of the sites arose over the millennia. While many of the round towers are now crumbling, and their function as antennae may no longer be operative, a field of holiness still surrounds the sites today.

ABOVE: The round tower on the Rock of Cashel is attached to a church that was built at a later date.

OPPOSITE: McCarthy's Tower, at the monastic site of Clonmacnoise, is one of two towers, the other being O'Rourke's Tower, which is missing its cap.

SKELLIG MICHAEL

Eight miles from Ballinskelligs Bay, off the tip of the
Iveragh Peninsula, is the island of Skellig Michael,
one of the most remote and enigmatic of the sacred
sites of Europe. In fact, Skellig Michael is the most
westerly in a line, sometimes called the Apollo St.
Michael axis, that was known thousands of years
before the advent of Christianity and which linked
the holy places of St. Michael's Mount, Mont St.-
Michel, Bourges, Perugia, Monte Gargano, Delphi,
Athens and Delos.

Legendary accounts of Skellig indicate its
importance in pagan times. The mythical early
invaders of Ireland, the Tuatha Dé Danaan, tell of
Milesius, whose son Irr was buried on Skellig in
around 1400 BC, while another tells of Daire

*BELOW & RIGHT: Skellig Michael or Great Skellig, a
UNESCO World Heritage site, is the larger of the two
Skellig islands, with two peaks rising to over 755ft
(230m) above sea level. An Irish Celtic monastery,
situated almost at the summit, was built in 588. The
monks lived in stone "beehive" huts (clochans), perched
above nearly vertical cliff walls.*

Domhain, a "king of the world," who stayed on the island. Little is known concerning the origins of the Celtic monastic settlement, but local lore associates it with St. Fionán, the Kerry saint, while other sources suggest that the first monks could have been Copts fleeing Roman and Byzantine persecution in the 6th century.

The first-known historical reference to the island comes from the end of the 5th century when the king of Munster, pursued by the king of Cashel, fled to Skellig. Another early mention of Skellig is to be found in the *Annals of Innisfallen* from AD 823, which tells how "Skellig was plundered by the heathen and Eitgal (the abbot) was carried off and he died of hunger on their hands."

From the early 9th century the Vikings repeatedly pillaged the monastery, killing many of its inhabitants. But somehow the monks endured, and legends tell that in 993, the Viking King Olaf Trygvasson (960s–1000), who introduced Christianity to Norway, was baptized by a hermit on Skellig Michael. The site was finally abandoned some time in the 13th century and many of the monks moved to the monastery of Ballinskelligs on the mainland.

The small cluster of six "beehive" huts, two oratories and small terraces are located 714ft (218m) above sea level, accessed by a steep climb of 600 stone steps. Facing south, and sheltered from the winds, the site was favored by hermits and monks wishing to live a quieter, more solitary life of prayer and contemplation. While the slate rock huts appear to be round from the outside, their insides are rectangular, with the walls curving inward to form a corbeled roof and with shelves and sleeping platforms built into the walls. Terraces around the huts and oratories were used to grow vegetables, which, along with fish and birds' eggs, were the

LEFT: Little Skellig, seen from Skellig Michael, is the smaller of the two Skellig islands. It is closed to the public, and accommodates Ireland's largest, and the world's second-largest, Northern Gannet colony, with almost 30,000 breeding pairs.

main food supply of the monks. There are three wells on the islet, whose area is only 44 acres (17.8 hectares). At a rocky crag, higher up on the south peak of Skellig, called the "Needle's Eye," is another oratory, inaccessible today, that continued to be used as a place of pilgrimage even after the monks had abandoned the island in the 13th century.

It is interesting to reflect on the identity of St. Michael, the patron saint of Skellig. St. Michael, venerated as an archangel in Jewish, Christian and Islamic teachings, is almost always depicted killing a "dragon" with a sword, and is said to carry the souls of the righteous to heaven. Scholars have commented on the similarity between the Celtic

notion of the "Isles of the Blessed," where the spirits of the deceased journeyed to the other world and Skellig's later dedication to St. Michael.

In this regard it is important to mention that a 13th-century German source claims that Skellig was the final scene of the battle between St. Patrick and the venomous snakes and devils that once plagued the island of Ireland. With the notion of St. Michael the Dragon-Slayer (dragons are synonymous with snakes in ancient mythologies), there is a clear indication of how folk memories of the old pagan religion persisted, even after it had been subsumed by the new Christian religion.

LOUGHCREW

Loughcrew, also called Slieve na Calliagh, is an
extensive collection of megalithic passage cairns
situated on the top of a range of hills on the
western border of County Meath. On one side of
the range are the lakes and lowlands of Cavan,
while the other side is bordered by the Boyne valley
and its rivers. The River Boyne, according to legend
a personification of Bóann (Bóinn), the White Cow
Goddess, is also a reflection of the Milky Way,
which alludes to the celestial dimension of this
sacred landscape and its importance as a portal to
the other world.

Loughcrew, with more than 30 chambered
cairns, encompasses the highest concentration of
ancient sacred architecture in all of Ireland (though
Carrowmore covers the largest area). Most of the
cairns, some of which are locked, are located on
two hills, Carnbane East and Carnbane West. The
hill of Carnbane East is also known as the "Hill of
the Hag" and the largest cairn on the hill was
supposedly her cave. Each of the hills and their
cairns have connections with ancient folkloric
stories of giants and heroes bewitched by fairy
women and goddesses.

The period of construction of the Loughcrew
cairns is believed to have begun as early as 4000 BC,
though exact dating has yet to be ascertained. One
interesting method of determining this is through
archeoastronomy or astro-archeology, which is the
investigation of the astronomical knowledge of
prehistoric cultures. Etensive studies have been
made, using this science, and the cairns' entrances
and passageways were found to be in alignment
with different periods in the solar calendar, such as
the solstices, equinoxes and cross-quarter days.

It is not currently known what were the exact
function of the passage cairns. Archeological
excavations have revealed burial remains in only a
few of them, and it is now believed that the cairns
and great mounds functioned not so much as burial
sites but as sacred places associated with life,
rebirth and regeneration. Some modern
researchers of the cairns, and of megalithic culture

in general, interpret the cairns as being the belly of
the earth goddess, complete with reproductive
organs, in which context it is important to consider
the solar alignments of the passageways leading into
the cairns. Perhaps, at ritually meaningful times of
the year, such as the solstices and equinoxes, when
the light of the sun penetrated directly along the

190

passageways, the megalithic people would utilize the cairns as places of ceremony whereby they would co-participate with the earth spirits in the continuing regeneration of life. Perhaps those periods of potent celestial influence were also used for initiation ceremonies and to awaken and amplify spiritual awareness.

ABOVE: Clusters of megalithic cairns are dotted around the Slieve na Callaigh hills c. Loughcrew, the main concentrations being on Carnbane East, where Cairn T is the centerpiece.

191

THE GRIANÁN OF AILEACH

The Grianán of Aileach comprises a group of ancient monuments in County Donegal, built on the Hill of Grianán which is 800ft (244m) high. Located not far from the Northern Ireland border, Grianán of Aileach is one of the finest stone ring forts in Ireland. From its hilltop, the fort commands impressive 360-degree views across Lough Swilly, Lough Foyle and the glorious countryside of the Inishowen Peninsula beyond.

The name Grianán of Aileach has variously been translated as "Stone Palace of the Sun," "Fortress of the Sun" and "Stone Temple of the Sun." Although heavily restored, there are no doubts as to the antiquity of the site, it being one of only five Irish locations marked on Ptolemy of Alexandria's 2nd-century map of the world.

The earthworks, thought to have been built in the late Bronze or early Iron Age, are the remains of a large ring fort that once enclosed the hilltop. Its ramparts have been eroded by time and only hints of their former glory remain, but recent surveys show that there were two sets of ramparts, an inner and outer. Both of the ramparts comprised a pair of banks, the total area enclosed by the outer boundary being about 5 acres (2 hectares). A hill fort with more than one enclosing wall is termed as multivallate and of the 50 or so known Irish examples, Grianán of Aileach is the only multivallate to be found in the north of the country.

The stone ring fort, also known as a caher or cashel, is thought to have been built during the early Christian era and from the 5th to the 12th centuries was the seat of the Northern Uí Néill, the rulers of the Fifth of Ulster.

The ruins of the cashel itself are described as a circular wall enclosing an area of 77ft 6in (23.6m) diameter. The wall had a height of 6ft (1.8m) with a breadth varying from 15ft (4.6m) to 11ft 6 in (3.5m). While not perpendicular, it inclined inward, indicating its similarity to most other Irish stone forts. The terrace is reached by flights of steps on either side of the entrance gateway

For centuries, the Northern Uí Néill alternated with the Southern Uí Néill, the rulers of the Fifth of Meath, for the kingship of Tara. In later centuries the term *Ard Ri*, or High King, superseded the kingship of Tara as a term for the overall ruler of Ireland and this term is often applied to the Uí Néill.

According to the Irish Annals, Grianán of Aileach was destroyed in 1101 by Muirchertach Ua Briain, king of Munster. In retaliation for the Uí Néill's destruction of his royal seat at Kincora, Ua Briain reportedly ordered each of his soldiers to take a stone from the fort so that Grianán would never be rebuilt. By around 1177, the Normans controlled large portions of lands once held by Aileach. According to some, Grianán of Aileach has been somewhat over-restored in places.

An Irish creation myth claims that the fortress was built by the great Dagda, of the Tuatha Dé Danann, as a grave for his son, Aeah, being in the center of the fortress which had been built around it. Whether such a grave existed is unknown, though a nearby tumulus could be a grave marker.

OPPOSITE & ABOVE: Grianán of Aileach is a prehistoric site in County Donegal. It contains one of the most impressive of all Ireland's ring forts.

KNOCK

Knock (Cnoc Mhuire), in County Mayo, is a major site of Roman Catholic pilgrimage and a National Shrine in Ireland where, it is claimed, there was a religious manifestation in 1879.

On the evening of August 21, 1879, 15 disparate people, whose ages ranged from five to 75, and included men, women, teenagers and children, witnessed what they claimed were apparitions of Our Lady, St. Joseph and St. John the Evangelist at the south gable end of the local small parish church of St. John the Baptist. Behind them, on a plain altar, appeared a cross and a lamb (the Lamb of God – Agnus Dei – a traditional image of Jesus as the perfect sacrifice for the redemption of mankind), surrounded by adoring angels. The manifestation lasted for about two hours.

The Blessed Virgin was described as standing a few feet above the ground. She was very beautiful and wore a white cloak, hanging in full folds about her body and fastened at the neck. On her head was a brilliant crown, the upper parts of which appeared to be composed of a series of sparkles or glittering crosses. She was described as being "deep in prayer," with her eyes turned toward heaven and her hands raised to the shoulders or a little higher, the palms inclined slightly toward the shoulders. One of the witnesses immediately went to kiss, what she thought were the feet of Our Lady, but there was nothing there, although the figure could still plainly be seen.

St. Joseph, also wearing white robes, stood at the Virgin's right hand, his head bent forward and turned toward the Virgin in an attitude of respect. St. John the Evangelist stood to the left of the Blessed Virgin. He was dressed in a long robe and wore a bishop's miter. He was partly turned away from the other figures, and appeared to be preaching, reading from a large, open book held in his left hand. To the left of St. John was an altar with a cross standing on it, in front of which was the Lamb of God.

Those who witnessed the multiple apparitions stood in the pouring rain for up to two hours reciting the Rosary, a traditional Catholic prayer dedicated to Our Lady. When the apparitions began there had been a good light, but although it subsequently became very dark, witnesses could still see the figures clearly, in that they appeared to be lit by a bright, whitish light. The apparitions did not flicker or move in any way. The witnesses reported that the ground around the figures remained completely dry during the manifestation, although the wind was blowing from the south. Afterwards, however, the ground at the gable end became wet and the gable dark.

To put the event in its historical context, the manifestation took place only nine years after the declaration of papal infallibility and shortly before the death of Archbishop MacHale, who led the resulting investigations. Two ecclesiastical commissions, one in 1879 and one in 1936, examined the events and the witnesses' reports and endorsed the genuineness of the appearances. The conclusions of these commissions permitted the establishment of Knock as a recognized site of Marian pilgrimage.

While neither accepting nor disputing what had allegedly occurred, but seeking to understand their cultural context, many noted the timing of the events: how, as at Lourdes and Fatima, the visitations had occurred at a time of immense cultural, social and economic change to people whose traditional way of life was under threat. In the 1870s, Ireland was undergoing a period of dramatic upheaval: some parts of the island had experienced what proved to be the last waves of a famine but which nevertheless rekindled memories of the Great Irish Famine of the late 1840s that had decimated the countryside. Depending on whether one accepted the veracity of the accounts or the religious beliefs underpinning them, they could be seen either as the delusions of a marginalized, traditional society, clinging to its old certainties or, in a Catholic religious context, as the appearance of the "Mother of God" to a people badly in need of her comfort and support.

OPPOSITE & OVERLEAF: The Marian shrine of Knock in County Mayo.

194

CARROWMORE

An Cheathrú Mhór, meaning the Great Quarter, is the largest and possibly the oldest megalithic cemetery in Ireland, predating Newgrange by 700 years. Carrowmore is ringed by mountains and stands on a low-lying gravel ridge at the center of a prehistoric, ritual landscape on the Cúil Irra Peninsula in County Sligo.

With an area of more than 1.5^2 miles ($3884982.2m^2$), Carrowmore comprises stone rings, dolmens and passage cairns. Evidence has been found of a Mesolithic presence dating from around 7500 BC and Goran Bürenholt, the Swedish archeologist, has suggested that one of the structures, known as 52A, may be as old as 5400 BC.

Presently, the site has more than 30 passage cairns and another 25 are known to have been destroyed since the early 1800s by workers quarrying stones and by treasure-hunters. The tombs (in their original state) are almost always "dolmen circles," i.e., small dolmens enclosed by boulder rings of 40–50ft (12–15m), each with a small leveling platform made of earth and stone, which may well be the secret of the dolmens' longevity. The combination of five of these orthostats, together with a capstone, encloses a pentagonal burial chamber. The boulder circles contain 30–40 boulders, usually of gneiss, the material of choice for the satellite tombs. Sometimes an inner boulder circle is present. Entrance stones, or passage stones, crude double rows of standing stones, emphasize the direction of

BELOW: Tomb 7 at Carrowmore is a burial chamber within a stone circle.

OPPOSITE: Carrowmore is dominated by the curbed tumulus of Misgán Méadbha (Medb's or Maeve's Cairn, Lump or Pimple) on the summit of Knocknarea.

the small monuments, which generally face toward the area of the central tomb. The "satellite" tombs or dolmens are distributed in a roughly oval shape measuring about 0.6 x 0.4 miles (1 x .6 km), with the largest cairn, called Listoghil, having been placed at the highest point at the center. Listoghil displays the characteristics typical of the Carrowmore tombs, i.e., short passage and small chamber, roofed by lintels rather than corbels. Listoghil stands at the highest point in the Carrowmore complex, about 164ft (50m) above sea level. Queen Medb's tomb, close by, on Knocknarea, has a cairn twice the diameter, and stands at about 33ft (10m): unopened but almost certainly containing a passage tomb, it is 180ft (55m) in diameter and over 33ft (10m)

high. It is surrounded by the remains of several tombs and cairns.

Almost all the burials at Carrowmore appear to have been cremations, with burials occurring only at Listoghil. It is apparent that the dead underwent a complex sequence of treatments, including excarnation and reburial. Grave goods include antler pins with mushroom-shaped heads and stone or clay balls, a fairly typical assemblage of the Irish passage-tomb tradition.

Some of the tombs and pits nearby contained shells, echoing the finds of shell middens found along the coast of Cúil Irra. The Carrowmore megaliths were sometimes re-used and re-shaped

by the people of Bronze Age and Iron Age times and remained focal points on the landscape long after they were built. The role of megaliths as monuments and focuses of ceremony and celebration, as well as markers on the landscape, is emphasized by archeologists, as opposed to earlier commentators, who called the monuments "tombs," regarding them simply as repositories for the dead or as markers where warriors had fallen.

Radiocarbon dates from the survey and excavation project in the 1970s, 80s and 90s by Professor Göran Bürenhult have caused controversy among archeologists, particularly dates from one of the tombs of 5,400 BC (before the perceived advent

of agriculture in Ireland). But were the tombs we see today built here this early? There have been objections, but the idea of Mesolithic tomb builders is still advocated by Bürenhult, although this contradicts the prevailing view which generally associates Neolithic farming societies with megalithic sites.

Supporters of the early dates sometimes point to similarly ancient dates attributed to chamber tombs in Brittany, where Mesolithic microliths have been found in association with at least one passage grave and some other very early dates in the Sligo area. Perhaps the key point is that Bürenhult's work, and that of later researchers, places the bulk

of the megalith building in Carrowmore at between 4000 and 3500 BC, which is more in keeping with Neolithic dating but still unusually early. It also challenged the idea that Irish prehistoric sites, such as Knowth and Newgrange, were the earliest in Ireland. Excavation of other tombs in the Cúil Irra area has indicated that, although different architectural styles were used, many were in fact contemporaneous with Carrowmore.

ABOVE: Listoghil, a megalithic tomb within Carrowmore. Queen Medb's tomb can clearly be seen on the summit of Knocknarea in the background.

201

DUN AENGUS

Dun Aengus or Dún Aonghasa is the most famous of several prehistoric forts located on the Aran Islands of County Galway. It is situated on Inishmore, at the edge of a 330ft (100m) high cliff. A popular tourist attraction, Dun Aengus is an important archeological site that also offers a spectacular view. It is not known when it was built, though it is now thought to date from the Iron Age.

Dun Aengus has been described as "the most magnificent barbaric monument in Europe." Its name, meaning "Aengus' Fort," refers to Aengus or Aonghus, who was a member of the Tuatha Dé Danann and probably a god of love, youth and poetic inspiration. He was the son of Bóann (the personification of the River Boyne) and the Dagda, with whom she had had an illicit affair.

The fort consists of a series of four concentric walls of dry-stone construction, its surviving

BELOW: One of the dry-stone walls of Dun Aengus fort.

OPPOSITE: View of the north coast of Inishmore, seen from Dun Aengus.

stonework being 13ft (4m) wide at some points. The original shape was presumably oval or D-shaped but parts of the cliff and fort have since collapsed into the sea. Outside the third ring of walls lies a defensive system of stone slabs, known as a *cheval de frise*, which consists of thousands of sharp pieces of limestone set upright in the ground to impede access, and which is still largely well-preserved. These ruins also feature a huge rectangular stone slab, the function of which is unknown.

Impressively large among prehistoric ruins, the outermost wall of Dun Aengus encloses an area of approximately 14 acres (6 hectares). Although clearly defensible, the particular location of the fort suggests that its primary purpose was religious and ceremonial rather than military. It may have been used for seasonal rites by the Druids, perhaps involving the bonfires that could be seen from the mainland of Ireland. The location also provides a view of as much as 75 miles (120km) of Atlantic coastline, which may have allowed a coastal trading highway to be controlled.

RIGHT: Dun Aengus is a vast site, probably used more for ceremonial than for military purposes.

CARROWKEEL

Known locally as "The Pinnacles," the Carrowkeel cairns are 15 miles (24km) south of Sligo on ridges in the Bricklieve Mountains. Fourteen cairns are to be found in the complex, and on the northern slope of the eastern ridge is a cluster of "hut circles," known as the Doonaveeragh Neolithic village.

Carrowkeel is believed to have been constructed between 3000 and 2000 BC, remaining in use until 1500 BC. The cairns, built of limestone with interior chambers roofed with large limestone slabs, range in size from 25–100ft (8–30m) in diameter. The site was used in Christian times as a burial place for unbaptized children. Carrowkeel was rapidly and very poorly excavated in 1911, often with the use of dynamite, and each of the cairns was assigned an identification letter.

Cairn G has a roof box above its doorway, which functions in a similar way to that in the enormous passage cairn of Newgrange. This allows sunlight to enter the cairn for a month either side of the summer solstice, and moonlight to enter for a month either side of the winter solstice. The cairn opens toward the most northerly point of the setting moon, a point which is reached only once in every 18.6 years. From Cairn K the sun can be seen to set, on both Samhain (also known as "All Saints' Day," November 1) and Imbolc (the beginning of the Celtic year on February 2), behind the sacred mountain of Croagh Patrick, 75 miles (120km) away to the southwest in County Mayo. At the rear of Cairn K there is a particular rock, known as the Croagh Patrick Stone, whose outline closely resembles that of the mountain, which demonstrates that the megalithic builders of ancient Ireland were keen observers of the celestial realm.

LEFT: Carrowkeel, a Neolithic passage tomb cemetery in the south of County Sligo, near Boyle, County Roscommon.

THE HOLY WELLS OF IRELAND

Holy wells were frequently former pagan sites of worship that later became Christianized. Any small water source, which had gained some significance in the folklore of the area where it was located might, over time, come to be attributed with healing powers through the numinous presence of its guardian spirit or Christian saint, or there may have been a ceremony or ritual that became centered on the well site itself. In Christian legend, the water is often said to have been made to flow by the action of a saint, a familiar theme, especially in the hagiography of Celtic saints. Where once a sacrifice may have taken place in the vicinity of a holy well, today a bride might make a good luck wish or a sick person take the waters in the hope of a cure. Often the Stations of the Cross are followed or a special mass is said in the vicinity. A ritual practice dating from prehistoric times, and continuing today, is that of circumambulation, or walking around the well, which must always be done in a clockwise direction.

The Celts, a grain-cultivating, cattle-raising people, exerted a strong religious influence on the native Irish. One of the features of Irish Celtic cosmogeny is the concept of the "power of place" (*genius loci*) or the belief that certain places possess a unique power that is curative and regenerative. In Ireland, this power of place is an essential element of the sacredness of a holy well.

Many myths attach themselves to sacred springs or holy wells, including those concerning erotic love, intoxication as wisdom, the location of such springs as being in the Otherworld, which can mean both the land of the dead as well as the land of eternal youth. The Otherworld is perceived to be a source of power and wisdom and is thought to be located beneath the earth, hidden in a mound, under the sea, in the far west, or on a plain hidden in a mist. These elements can be found in the Fenian Cycle, the "Brown Bull of Cooley," "Niall and the Hag at the Well," among others. Always, the emphasis among the Celtic earth-centered

people was of cyclic regeneration rather than the linear movement or evolution of the historical. Even today, the "rounds" made at various of these holy wells embodies tradition rooted in antiquity. St. Patrick's Well in Ardfert, County Kerry, for example, contains an altar with saints' heads worn away by the constant rubbing of pilgrims' fingers in search of healing. St. Ciaran's Well, at Clonmacnoise, County Offaly, has three stone heads that are routinely kissed and marked as pilgrims make their rounds or "patrons." A Booley stone activates St. Erc's Well at Listowel, County Kerry, this being a well marked by a pre-Christian standing stone.

There are different types of wells. Prior to the coming of St. Patrick, sacred springs reflected Celtic earth-centered spirituality, but after Patrick there was a shift to "Christianize" the pilgrimages and practices associated with the wells. A crossover symbol between the ancient Celtic and the new Christian culture is the fish. Many wells are reputed to contain sacred trout or salmon, which may or may not be the saint for whom that well is named, and as there was a shift from the ancient Celtic sacred springs to St. Patrick wells, so there was a shift from Brigid wells to Lady wells. Before St. Brigid was canonized, there had been an earlier Brigid who was a daughter/lover/wife of the Dagda, one of the Otherworld lords. Thus she was the Otherworld queen, venerated for her attributes of fertility and healing. She was especially identified with milk, dairy products and the cow, also for her patronage of the blacksmith's fire.

OPPOSITE: St. Patrick's holy well is to be found 2 miles (3.2km) to the southwest of Clonmel in County Waterford. It occupies an early Christian site beside a ruined 17th-century church. In the center of the sacred healing pool stands an early Christian cross.

TOBARNALT

A sacred place of the Celts, this grove and its holy well, located about three miles southeast of Sligo town, were later adopted by St. Patrick and re-dedicated to Christianity. The well of cold, clear water bubbles up at the foot of a steep rock wall and flows towards Loch Gill in the distance. Near the center of the grove of trees, which surrounds the well, and just below the well itself, there is a healing stone with a depression at one end where a person can lean their back to cure a back pain.

Impressed on this stone are four indentations, said to have been left by St. Patrick, and by resting one's fingers on them, some of the saint's powers are said to be transferred.

The Christian Pattern day (pattern indicating the primary day of pilgrimage visitation) is the final Sunday in July each year. Just off the shore of Loch Gill there is an island called Inishmore, which, besides Dun Aengus fort, contains the ruins of an ancient church.

SAINT DECLAN'S WELL

Declan's birthplace is said to be Drumroe, near Cappoquin in County Waterford, and he is thought to have been born some time in the 5th century AD. He is said to have completed his studies for the priesthood in Rome, where he was ordained by the pope and eventually became a bishop. On returning to Ireland, Declan met St. Patrick, and the two decided between themselves what the sphere of their mission in Ireland should be. On Patrick's instructions, Declan founded the monastery which lies near the Irish coast in the southeast of the kingdom of the Déisi Muman and, having obtained Patrick's blessing, went on to convert the Déisi to Christianity.

St. Declan founded the monastery at Ardmore (Aird Mhór, meaning "Great Height") in County Waterford, and it is believed to be one of the oldest of its kind in Ireland.

St. Declan's Well, which was a place of healing in pagan times, is located on the headland above the

town of Ardmore, where the church and round tower stand, and which is said to be one of the most beautiful in the whole of Ireland. The well served as a bapistry to the early Christian missionaries, and St. Declan is sometimes regarded as the father of Christianity in Ireland. St. Declan's Day is July 24.

OTHER WELLS WORTH VISITING
CLARE

St. Brigid's Well, Liscannor

Eye Well, The Burren

Tooth Well, The Burren

Margaret's Well, Ennis

St. Augustine's Well, Kilshanny

CORK

St. Olan's Well, Aghbullogue

Tobrid Well, Millstreet

Ballinspittle

Inchigeela

Sunday's Well and Mary's Well, Walshestown

St. Finbar's Well, Gougane Barra

KERRY

Well of the Wethers, Ardfert

St. Dahlin's, Ballyheige

St. John's Well, Dingle

St. Erc's Well, Listowel

St. Eoin's Well, Listowel

St. Michael's Well, Ballymore West

Lady Well, Ballyheige

OPPOSITE: Predating the coming of Christianity to Ireland in the 5th century, the Tobernalt holy well is a place of serenity and quiet contemplation.

RIGHT: Holy wells such as this one, can be found all over Ireland.

KILDARE

Earl's Well, Kildare

St. Brigid's Well, Kildare

Father Moore's Wel, Kildare

MEATH

Tobar Patraic, Ardmulchan

St. John's Well, Warrenstown

Tara (Neamnach, Toberfin, and Leacht), Castlebye

ROSCOMMON

Tober Oglalla, Tulsk

St. Lassair's Well, Lough Meelagh

St. Attracta's Well, Monasteraden

SLIGO

St. Brigid's Well, Cliffony

Tullaghan Well, Tullaghan

St. Patrick's Well, Dromard

St. Patrick's Well, Aughris

The Bog, The Culleens

STANDING STONES & DOLMENS

POULNABRONE DOLMEN

Ireland's most photographed dolmen sits in the heart of the world-famous Burren plateau of northwest County Clare in what is the finest example of a karstic terrain, with a full assemblage of the curious landforms and subterranean drainage systems characteristic of such limestone regions. The Poulnabrone Dolmen is a portal tomb dating back to the Neolithic period, probably between 4200–2900 BC. It is situated 5 miles (8km) south of Ballyvaughan in the parish of Carran, 6 miles (10km) northwest of Kilnaboy.

A crack was discovered in the dolmen's eastern portal stone in 1985 and, following the resulting collapse, the dolmen was dismantled and the cracked stone replaced. Excavations made at this time revealed that between 16 and 22 adults and six children had been buried under the monument, while a newborn baby had been interred in the portico, just outside the entrance. Personal items buried with the dead included a polished stone axe, a bone pendant, quartz crystals, weapons and pottery. With its dominating position on the limestone landscape of the Burren, the tomb was thought to have been a center for ceremony and ritual until well into the Celtic period, or it may have served as a territorial marker in the Neolithic landscape.

The dolmen is made of limestone slabs typical of the many other Bronze Age wedge tombs found in the locality. It consists of a 12-ft (4-m), thin, slab-like tabular capstone, supported by two slender portal stones, which lifts the capstone 6ft (1.8m) from the ground, creating a chamber in a 30-ft (9-m) low cairn. The cairn helped stabilize the tomb chamber, and would have been no higher during the Neolithic period. The entrance faces north and is crossed by a low sill stone.

BROWNESHILL DOLMEN

The Browneshill Dolmen (Dolmain Chnoc an Bhrúnaigh in Irish) is a megalithic portal tomb situated 1.9 miles (3km) east of Carlow, in County Carlow, Ireland. It is the county's most prominant feature, yet no one knows who actually built it. The capstone weighs an estimated 100 tons and is reputed to be the heaviest in Europe. The tomb is listed as a National Monument.

The dolmen was built between 4000 and 3000 BC by some of the earliest farmers to inhabit the island. It is also known as Browneshill Portal Tomb, so-called because the entrance to the burial chamber was flanked by two large upright stones (orthostats) supporting the granite capstone, or roof, of the chamber. The capstone is thought to have been covered by an earthen mound and a gate stone blocked the entrance. At Browneshill both portal stones and the gate stone are still in situ, the capstone lying on top of the portals and gate stone and sloping to the ground away from the entrance. Not much additional information is available concerning Browneshill because it has never been excavated. A fourth upright stands close by and could be the remains of a forecourt. The extent of the chamber cannot be determined.

PAGES 212-213: Poulnabrone Dolmen.

BELOW: The Kernanstown Cromlech, popularly called the Browneshill Dolmen, is situated on a hill on which sits the former estate house of the Browne family, from which the hill takes its name.

OPPOSITE: Kilclooney Dolmen is a particularly fine example of a portal tomb.

KILCLOONEY DOLMEN

Prominent on the skyline 4 miles (6km) north-northwest of Ardara, in Country Donegal, Kilclooney is an exceptionally fine portal tomb, built more than 4000 years ago and probably older than Stonehenge on Salisbury plain in England. It consists of a massive roofstone resting on two uprights with a supportive backstone. Originally there would have been other slabs of stone creating a walled-in effect, but which are now missing.

There is some evidence to suggest that the dolmen was surrounded by a mound of earth, with more than one tomb included in the cairn. There is a second, smaller portal tomb at the Kilclooney

site that has not been excavated, and it is distinctly possible that the two dolmens were built in more than one phase. Fragments of Neolithic pottery are the only recorded finds. A modern field wall separates the two, which were evidently mounded over by the same east-facing cairn, traces of which still remain.

The tomb is substantially complete. A low sill stone, set between the 6ft (2m) high portals closes off the chamber entrance. The lower end of the capstone does not rest directly on the backtone, as is usually the case, but is supported instead by a small intermediate stone whose function may have been to give increased height to the chamber.

215

BEAGHMORE STONE CIRCLES

Beaghmore is a complex of early Bronze Age megalithic features 8.5 miles (14km) northwest of Cookstown, County Tyrone, on the southeast edge of the Sperrin Mountains. It has been suggested that the name comes from Bheitheach Mhór, meaning "big place of birch trees," a name reflecting how the area was once a woodland site. It is possible that Neolithic occupation and cultivation preceded the erection of the burial cairns and ceremonial circles and alignments, and some irregular lines and heaps of boulders, resembling field-fences or field-clearance, may have predated the ritual structures.

Discovered when cutting peat during the 1940s, the site at Beaghmore consists of seven stone circles, with all the rings being associated with cairns with a stone row running toward them. At some stage peat started to form over the site, and it may conceivably be that the cairns and rows were erected in a futile propitiatory attempt to restore fertility to the soil by attracting back the fading sun. There are seven low stone circles of different sizes, six of which are paired, with 12 cairns and 10 stone rows. The circles are between 33 and 66ft (10 and 20m) in diameter, and are associated with earlier burial cairns and alignments of stone rows leading toward them.

The stones are small with a few more than 1.6ft (5m) in height and the circles are distorted, suggesting they are related to the curbs surrounding some megalithic tombs. The singular circle is distinguished from the paired circles by its slightly larger stones. It is also unique in that the interior of the circle is filled with more than 800 small stones, which have been placed upright within the circle and are known as "the dragon's teeth."

Most of these circles have small stone alignments touching them at a tangent. The site also includes a dozen small stone cairns, frequently covering a cremation burial. Each of the three pairs of stone circles have a small cairn placed in between. A typical feature of the stone rows is a high and low arrangement where short rows of tall stones run beside much longer rows of small stones. The stone rows radiate from the circles in a roughly northeast direction.

The site also consists of low banks of small stones running below, and possibly pre-dating, the other structures which may have been field walls in the Neolithic period. Excavation has revealed that the site overlays a Neolithic cultivation site, and it is thought that the stones may have been erected in response to deteriorating soil fertility and the encroachment of peat. Following excavation, a system of drainage channels had to be laid to prevent the stones from being reclaimed once again by the bog.

The site could possibly have marked a focal point for religious or social gatherings. Some archeologists believe that the circles have been constructed in relation to the rising of the sun at the solstice, or to record the movements of the sun and moon acting as observatories for particular lunar, solar or stellar events. Three of the stone rows point to the sunrise at the time of the solstice, and another is aligned toward moonrise at the same period. Most of the remains at Beaghmore, however, do not indicate very accurate alignments upon specific astronomical features.

Because of the number of stone cairns on the site, it is possible that at least part of the function of the site was burial, and some cairns have been found to contain cremated human remains. But not all the cairns have burial remains and they could have had other purposes.

OPPOSITE: Beaghmore is a large early Bronze Age site consisting of stone circles, cairns and alignments.

BALLYCROVANE

Just over 600ft (180m) southeast of the coastguard
station at Ballycrovane's harbor, on the Beara
Peninsula, lies this impressive standing stone which,
at 17ft (5m) high, looks almost like a piece of
modern sculpture.

The purpose of standing stones is as enigmatic
as that of stone circles; some suggest they may have
marked burials, others explain them as markers
along prehistoric trackways. The Ballycrovane
standing stone was possibly erected to mark one of
the westernmost points of Ireland.

Ballycrovane, the tallest Ogham stone in the
world, bears an inscription in this ancient British
and Irish alphabet: MAQI-DECCEDDAS AVI
TURANIAS, translated as "Of the son of Deich,
descendant of Torainn."

BELTANY

On the leveled summit of Tops Hill, about 2 miles
south of the village of Raphoe, is this fine stone
circle, one of the few in northwest Ireland. The
name Beltany suggests that the pagan festival of
Beltane (May Day) was celebrated on the site.

The ring is 145ft (44m) in diameter and still
consists of 64 stones, though there were originally
80 or more. The style is similar to the circles in the
Carrowmore cemetery, and it is possible that
Beltany is a transitional ring between late passage
tombs and early stone circles.

The circle, substantially older than the Iron
Age, also incorporates a tumulus, which may be the

remains of a pillaged cairn, and some theories claim that the whole site should really be classified as a round cairn with the orthostats comprising a curbing.

The site was disturbed at the beginning of the century causing many of the stones, which have an average height of 6ft (1.8m), to lean outward at acute angles. When Oliver Davies visited the site in the late 1930s, he reported that "The platform had been recently and unscientifically excavated, and had been left in dreadful confusion."

To the east-northeast is a triangular slab whose inner face is decorated with cupmarks. There is also one 6ft 3-in high stone standing outside the circle, at about 66ft (20m) to the southeast.

There are some theories of astronomical alignments concerning the circle, the most persuasive being that from the high west-southwest pillar to the cupmarked slab whose pointed top provides a sighting point toward the hill-summit of Tullyrap, a few miles away.

OPPOSITE: The impressively tall Ogham stone, near to Ballycrovane in Country Cork.

ABOVE: Beltany is a transitional stone circle on the summit of Topps Hill, near Raphoe, County Donegal.

INDEX

INDEX

ACKNOWLEDGEMENTS

COVER IMAGES
Front cover: Shutterstock Images LLC © Pecold
Back cover: Shutterstock Images LLC © Jane McIlroy

The following photographs supplied courtesy of Shutterstock Images LLC © by the following photographers:- Accent: page 54 (insert). Agnieszka Guzowska: pages 22-23, 104-105, 116-117 (background). Aleks.K: pages 134-135. Alexmcguttie: page 34 left. Algol: page 92-93. Andreas Juergensmeier: pages 186-187. Andrei Verner: page 112-113 (background). Andrey Valerevich: page 107 below. Anthony Hall: pages 88-89, 206-207. Arthur Bogacki: page 208. Basel 101658: page 95. Bill McKelvie: page 71 (insert). Birgit Urban: pages 188-189. Bo Valentino: page 14 top right. Brian Dunne: pages 38-39. Bruce McQueen: page 109 right. Christy Nicholas: page 215. Claudia Naerdemann: page 111 (insert). Collpicto: page 47. Cyborgwitch: pages 122-123. Czesznak Zsolt: page 139. DeCe: page 112 (insert below). Donal Mullins: page 55. Ecoventurestravel: page 202. Eduard Kyslynskyy: pages 20-21. Eireann: pages 74, 167, 180. Ellerslie: pages 17, 143. EML: page 73. Esteban De Armas: page 102 below. Evokzo: page 138. Fer Gregory: page 121 (insert). Fractalgr: page 92 left. Gabriela Insuratelu: page 183. Heartland: page 103. Henry E. StammIV: pages 70-71 (background). Iarislav Neliubov: page 118 (insert). Igor Kovalchu: page 10. iLight Foto: pages 52, 66. Incredible-Moments (crosses): page 1, 3, 10, 46, 86, 96, 126, 144. Irabel8: pages 14-15 (background). Jaimie Duplass: page 132. James R. Hearn: page 154. Jane McIlroy: pages 140 below, 199. Jean-Noel Latargue: page 7 below. Jeffrey T. Kreulen: page 113 (insert). Jjones55: page 193. Joe Gough: page 142 below. John A Cameron: page 30 left. Jurand: page 64 (insert). Kevin King: page 19 below. Krechet: page 214. Lario Tus: page 131. Lauren Adgie: page 181 right. Lauri Barr: page 136. LiliGraphic: page 46 (background). Linda Bucklin: page 119. Lukasz Pajor: pages 212-213. Maceofoto: page 6 right. Madam Evangelista: page 70 (insert). Mariait: pages 128-129.

Markus Gann: pages 48-49. MartaP: page 36. Matthi: pages 40-41 below, 58-59, 126-127, 141 below. Max Nagoruyy: pages 20-21 (background). Michaelupthebanner: page 184-185. Misa Maric: pages 172-173. MMacKillop: page 27 above. M Reel: pages 44-45, 158. Neil Forrester: pages 18-19 (background), 150-151. Nici Kuehl: page 114-115. Norman Pogson: page 107 above. Olinchuk: page 41 above. Panaspics: pages 56-57, 178 right. Patrimono Designs Limited: page 14 above left. Patrick Niall Dunne: page 54 (background). Patriyk Kosmider: pages 2, 64-65 (background), 124-125 (background), 155, 156-157, 164-165. Paul Cowan: page 195. Paul R Seftel: pages 50-51. Paul Wilkinson: page 37. Pecold: pages 7 below, 12-13, 35, 53, 176-177. PHB.CZ (Richard Semik): pages 90 below, 133, 159, 168-169, 170, 217. Pierre Leclerc: pages 42-43, 160-161. Piotr Gatlik: pages 76-77. Pyma: page 144 above. Rarena: page 181 left. Ratalstachura: page 75. Richard Melichar: page 182. Robert Adrian Hilman: page 56 left. Rowan McLaughlin: page 29. Rund Morijn Photographer: pages 32-33 (background). Sandra Cunningham: page 116 (insert). Sandy S: page 184 left. Sarah777: pages 26-27 below. Seamartini Graphics: pages 130, 150 left, 152 left, 165 right, 168 left, 178 left, 187. right, 194 left, 208 left, 211 right. Sergey Prygov: page 114 left. Snec: page 62 (background). Spectrumblue: page 149. Thomas Barrat: page 162 below. TSpider: page 24-25 (background). UnaPhoto: pages 11, 148. Vadim: page 120 (insert). Vaide Seskanskiene: pages 4-5. Vector Shots: page 118 (background). Walshfotos: pages 8-9, 79, 80-81, 100-101, 110-111 (background), 120-121. (background), 163, 179. Warren Price Photography: page 137. Wavebreakmedia Ltd.: pages 60-61. Yellowj: page 125 (insert). Zbynek Burival: page 171. Zdanchuk Svetland: pages 140 above, 142 above. The following images supplied by Flickr/Creative Commons www.creativecommons.org and the following photographers: BA Banks: page 210. Jow King: page 96. Kay Atherton: page 68 left. Lian Moloney: pages 68-69. Wikimedia Commons: Brholden: page 145. Cath: page 84. Dunlavin

ACKNOWLEDGEMENTS

Green: pages 203, 204-205. Gunter ClaBen: pages 174-175 below. Jean-Noel Latargue: page 7 above. HR Millar: page 26 above. Logopin: pages 200-201. Mkooiman: pages 15, 46. Nemoi: page 146-147. Piedra del Destino: page 86. Peter Ribbans: page 218 left . PKean: pages 196-197. Public Domain/Wikimedia: pages 16 both, 18, 28 both, 31 right, 32 above, 34 right, 62 (insert), 63, 65 (insert), 67, 72 all, 82, 83 both, 85, 87, 90 above, 91, 94 both, 97, 98-99, 102 above, 106 both, 108-109, 110 all, 112 (insert above), 141 above, 144 below, 146 left, 152-153, 162 above, 192, 198, 218-219. Sakrajda: page 175 above. Thomas Crofton Croker: page 6 left. William Murphy: page 25. William T Whyte: pages 190-191.